C-2
ISBN 0-8373-0002-9

THE PASSBOOK® SERIES

PASSBOOKS®

FOR

CAREER OPPORTUNITIES

ACCOUNT CLERK

National Learning Corporation

212 Michael Drive, Syosset, New York 11791

(516) 921-8888

Copyright © 1998 by

National Learning Corporation

212 Michael Drive, Syosset, New York 11791
(516) 921-8888

PRINTED IN THE UNITED STATES OF AMERICA

PASSBOOK®
NOTICE

PASSBOOK SERIES®

THE *PASSBOOK SERIES®* has been created to prepare applicants and candidates for the ultimate academic battlefield—the examination room.

At some time in our lives, each and every one of us may be required to take an examination—for validation, matriculation, admission, qualification, registration, certification, or licensure.

Based on the assumption that every applicant or candidate has met the basic formal educational standards, has taken the required number of courses, and read the necessary texts, the *PASSBOOK SERIES®* furnishes the one special preparation which may assure passing with confidence, instead of failing with insecurity. Examination questions—together with answers—are furnished as the basic vehicle for study so that the mysteries of the examination and its compounding difficulties may be eliminated or diminished by a sure method.

This book is meant to help you pass your examination provided that you qualify and are serious in your objective.

The entire field is reviewed through the huge store of content information which is succinctly presented through a provocative and challenging approach—the question-and-answer method.

A climate of success is established by furnishing the correct answers at the end of each test.

You soon learn to recognize types of questions, forms of questions, and patterns of questioning. You may even begin to anticipate expected outcomes.

You perceive that many questions are repeated or adapted so that you gain acute insights, which may enable you to score many sure points.

You learn how to confront new questions, or types of questions, and to attack them confidently and work out the correct answers.

You note objectives and emphases, and recognize pitfalls and dangers, so that you may make positive educational adjustments.

Moreover, you are kept fully informed in relation to new concepts, methods, practices, and directions in the field.

You discover that you are actually taking the examination all the time: you are preparing for the examination by "taking" an examination, not by reading extraneous and/or supererogatory textbooks.

In short, this PASSBOOK®, used directedly, should be an important factor in helping you to pass your test.

ARITHMETIC

EXAMINATION SECTION

CONTENTS

———

CLERICAL ABILITIES TEST

EXAMINATION SECTION

CONTENTS

———

NAME and NUMBER COMPARISON

CONTENTS

NAME AND NUMBER CHECKING

CONTENTS

———

CODING

EXAMINATION SECTION

CONTENTS

———

BASIC FUNDAMENTALS OF BOOKKEEPING

CONTENTS

ACCOUNT CLERK

DUTIES
Receives remittances by mail or in person; verifies amount, computes interest and penalties and posts to book or original entry; assists in maintaining labor, material and operational cost records; issues receipts for monies received; classifies constantly recurring receipts and expenditures and distributes costs according to prescribed code; operates computing, calculating, check writing and other office machines.

SUBJECT OF EXAMINATION
The written test will be designed to test for knowledge, skills, and/or abilities in such areas as:
1. Clerical operations with letters and numbers;
2. Arithmetic computation; and
3. Arithmetic reasoning.

———

HOW TO TAKE A TEST

I. YOU MUST PASS AN EXAMINATION

A. *WHAT EVERY CANDIDATE SHOULD KNOW*

   Examination applicants often ask us for help in preparing for the written test. What can I study in advance? What kinds of questions will be asked? How will the test be given? How will the papers be graded?

   As an applicant for a civil service examination, you may be wondering about some of these things. Our purpose here is to suggest effective methods of advance study and to describe civil service examinations.

   Your chances for success on this examination can be increased if you know how to prepare. Those "pre-examination jitters" can be reduced if you know what to expect. You can even experience an adventure in good citizenship if you know why civil service examinations are given.

B. *WHY ARE CIVIL SERVICE EXAMINATIONS GIVEN?*

   Civil service examinations are important to you in two ways. As a citizen, you want public jobs filled by employees who know how to do their work. As a job-seeker, you want a fair chance to compete for that job on an equal footing with other candidates. The best known means of accomplishing this two-fold goal is the competitive examination.

   Examinations are widely publicized throughout the nation. They may be administered for jobs in federal, state, city, municipal, town, or village governments or agencies.

   Any citizen may apply, with some limitations, such as the age or residence of applicants. Your experience and education may be reviewed to see whether you meet the requirements for the particular examination. When these requirements exist, they are reasonable and are applied consistently to all applicants. Thus, a competitive examination may cause you some uneasiness now, but it is your privilege and safeguard.

C. *HOW ARE CIVIL SERVICE EXAMINATIONS DEVELOPED?*

   Examinations are carefully written by trained technicians who are specialists in the field known as "psychological measurement," in consultation with recognized authorities in the field of work that the test will cover. These experts recommend the subject matter areas or skills to be tested; only those knowledges or skills important to your success on the job are included. The most reliable books and source materials available are used as references. Together, the experts and technicians judge the difficulty level of the questions.

   Test technicians know how to phrase questions so that the problem is clearly stated. Their ethics do not permit "trick" or "catch" questions. Questions may have been tried out on sample groups, or subjected to statistical analysis, to determine their usefulness.

   Written tests are often used in combination with performance tests, ratings of training and experience, and oral interviews. All of these measures combine to form the best known means of finding the right man for the right job.

II. HOW TO PASS THE WRITTEN TEST

A. *NATURE OF THE EXAMINATION*

To prepare intelligently for civil service examinations, you should know how they differ from school examinations you have taken. In school you were assigned certain definite pages to read or subjects to cover. The examination questions were quite detailed and usually emphasized memory. Civil service examinations, on the other hand, try to discover your present ability to perform the duties of a position, plus your potentiality to learn these duties. In other words, a civil service examination attempts to predict how successful you will be. Questions cover such a broad area that they cannot be as minute and detailed as school examination questions.

In the public service similar kinds of work, or positions, are grouped together in one "class." This process is known as "position-classification." All the positions in a class are paid according to the salary range for that class. One class title covers all these positions, and they are all tested by the same examination.

B. *FOUR BASIC STEPS*

1. Study the Announcement.--How, then, can you know what subjects to study? Our best answer is: "Learn as much as possible about the class of positions for which you have applied." The examination will test the knowledge, skills, and abilities needed to do the work.

Your most valuable source of information about the position you want is the official announcement of the examination. This announcement lists the training and experience qualifications. Check these standards and apply only if you come reasonably close to meeting them.

The brief description of the position in the examination announcement offers some clues to the subjects which will be tested. Think about the job itself. Review the duties in your mind. Can you perform them, or are there some in which you are rusty? Fill in the blank spots in your preparation.

Many jurisdictions preview the written test in the examination announcement by including a section called "Knowledge and Abilities Required," "Scope of Examination," or some similar heading. Here you will find out specifically what fields will be tested.

2. Review Your Own Background.-- Once you learn in general what the position is all about, and what you need to know to do the work, ask yourself which subjects you already know fairly well and which need improvement. You may wonder whether to concentrate on improving your strong areas or on building some background in your fields of weakness. When the announcement has specified "some knowledge" or "considerable knowledge," or has used adjectives such as "beginning principles of ...." or "advanced .....methods," you can get a clue as to the number and difficulty of questions to be asked in any given field. More questions, and hence broader coverage, would be included for those subjects which are more important in the work. Now weigh your strengths and weaknesses against the job requirements and prepare accordingly.

3. Determine the Level of the Position.-- Another way to tell how intensively you should prepare is to understand the level of the job for which you are applying. Is it the entering level? In other words, is this the position in which beginners in a field of work are hired? Or is it an intermediate or advanced level? Sometimes this is indicated by such words as "Junior" or "Senior" in the class title.Other jurisdictions use Roman numerals to designate the level: Clerk I,

Clerk II, for example. The word "Supervisor" sometimes appears in the title. If the level is not indicated by the title, check the description of duties. Will you be working under very close supervision, or will you have responsibility for independent decisions in this work?

4. Choose Appropriate Study Materials.-- Now that you know the subjects to be examined and the relative amount of each subject to be covered, you can choose suitable study materials. For beginning level jobs, or even advanced ones, if you have a pronounced weakness in some aspect of your training, read a modern, standard textbook in that field. Be sure it is up-to-date and has general coverage. Such books are normally available at your library, and the librarian will be glad to help you locate one. For entry level positions, questions of appropriate difficulty are chosen -- neither highly advanced questions, nor those too simple. Such questions require careful thought but not advanced training.

If the position for which you are applying is technical or advanced, you will read more advanced, specialized material. If you are already familiar with the basic principles of your field, elementary textbooks would waste your time. Concentrate on advanced textbooks and technical periodicals. Think through the concepts and review difficult problems in your field.

These are all general sources. You can get more ideas on your own initiative, following these leads. For example, training manuals and publications of the government agency which employs workers in your field can be useful, particularly for technical and professional positions. A letter or visit to the government department involved may result in more specific study suggestions, and certainly will provide you with a more definite idea of the exact nature of the position you are seeking.

II. KINDS OF TESTS

Tests are used for purposes other than measuring knowledge and ability to perform specified duties. For some positions, it is equally important to test ability to make adjustments to new situations or to profit from training. In others, basic mental abilities not dependent upon information are essential. Questions which test these things may not appear as pertinent to the duties of the position as those which test for knowledge and information. Yet they are often highly important parts of a fair examination. For very general questions, it is almost impossible to help you direct your study efforts. What we can do is to point out some of the more common of these general abilities needed in public service positions and describe some typical questions.

1. General Information

Broad, general information has been found useful for predicting job success in some kinds of work. This is tested in a variety of ways, from vocabulary lists to questions about current events. Basic background in some field of work, such as sociology or economics, may be sampled in a group of questions. Often these are principles which have become familiar to most persons through "exposure" rather than through formal training. It is difficult to advise you how to study for these questions; being alert to the world around you is our best suggestion.

2. Verbal Ability

An example of an ability needed in many positions is verbal or language ability. Verbal ability is, in brief, the ability to use and understand words. Vocabulary and grammar tests are typical measures of this ability. "Reading comprehension" or "paragraph interpretation" questions are common in many kinds of civil service tests. You are given a paragraph of written material and asked to find its central meaning.

3. Numerical Ability

Number skills can be tested by the familiar arithmetic problem, by checking paired lists of numbers to see which are alike and which are different, or by interpreting charts and graphs. In the latter test, a graph may be printed in the test booklet which you are asked to use as the basis for answering questions.

4. Observation

A popular test for law-enforcement positions is the observation test. A picture is shown to you for several minutes, then taken away. Questions about the picture test your ability to observe both details and larger elements.

5. Following Directions

In many positions in the public service, the employee must be able to carry out written instructions dependably and accurately. You may be given a chart with several columns, each column listing a variety of information. The questions require you to carry out directions involving the information given in the chart.

6. Skills and Aptitudes

Performance tests effectively measure some manual skills and aptitudes. When the skill is one in which you are trained, such as typing or shorthand, you can practice. These tests are often very much like those given in business school or high school courses. For many of the other skills and aptitudes, however, no short-time preparation can be made. Skills and abilities natural to you or that you have developed throughout your lifetime are being tested.

Many of the general questions just described provide all the data needed to answer the questions and ask you to use your reasoning ability to find the answers. Your best preparation for these tests, as well as for tests of facts and ideas, is to be at your physical and mental best. You, no doubt, have your own methods of getting into an exam-taking mood and keeping "in shape." The next section lists some ideas on this subject.

IV. KINDS OF QUESTIONS

Only rarely is the "essay" question, which you answer in narrative form, used in civil service tests. Civil service tests are usually of the short-answer type. Full instructions for answering these questions will be given to you at the examination. But in case this is your first experience with short-answer questions and separate answer sheets, here is what you need to know.

1. Multiple-Choice Questions

Most popular of the short-answer questions is the "multiple-choice" or "best-answer" question. It can be used, for example, to test for factual knowledge, ability to solve problems, or judgment in meeting situations found at work.

A multiple-choice question is normally one of three types:

(1) It can begin with an incomplete statement followed by several possible endings. You are to find the one ending which *best* completes the statement, although some of the others may not be entirely wrong.

(2) It can also be a complete statement in the form of a question which is answered by choosing one of the statements listed.

(3) It can be in the form of a problem -- again you select the best answer.

Here is an example of a multiple-choice question with a discussion which should give you some clues as to the method for choosing the right answer.

SAMPLE QUESTION:

When an employee has a complaint about his assignment, the action which will *best* help him overcome his difficulty is

    (A) to discuss his difficulty with his co-workers
    (B) to take the problem to the head of the organization
    (C) to take the problem to the person who gave him the assignment
    (D) to say nothing to anyone about his complaint

In answering this question you should study each of the choices to find which is best. Consider choice (A). Certainly an employee may discuss his complaint with fellow employees, but no change or improvement can result, and the complaint remains unsolved. Choice (B) is a poor choice since the head of the organization probably does not know what assignment you have been given, and taking your problem to him is known as "going over the head" of the supervisor. The supervisor, or person who made the assignment, is the person who can clarify it or correct any injustice. Choice (C) is, therefore, correct. To say nothing, as in choice (D), is unwise. Supervisors have an interest in knowing the problems employees are facing, and the employee is seeking a solution to his problem.

  2. True-False Questions

The "true-false" or "right-wrong" form of question is sometimes used. Here a complete statement is given. Your problem is to decide whether the statement is right or wrong.

SAMPLE QUESTION:

A person-to-person long distance telephone call costs less than a station-to-station call to the same city.

This question is wrong, or "false," since person-to-person calls are more expensive.

This is not a complete list of all possible question forms, although most of the others are variations of these common types. You will always get complete directions for answering questions. Be sure you understand *how* to mark your answers -- ask questions until you do.

V. RECORDING YOUR ANSWERS

For an examination with very few applicants, you may be told to record your answers in the test booklet itself. Separate answer sheets are much more common. If this separate answer sheet is to be scored by machine -- and this is often the case -- it is highly important that you mark your answers correctly in order to get credit.

An electric test-scoring machine is often used in civil service offices because of the speed with which papers can be scored. Machine-scored answer sheets must be marked with a special pencil, which will be given to you. This pencil has a high graphite content which responds to the electrical scoring machine. As a matter of fact, stray dots may register as answers, so do not let your pencil rest on the answer sheet while you are pondering the correct answer. Also, if your pencil lead breaks or is otherwise defective, ask for another.

Since the answer sheet will be dropped in a slot in the scoring machine, be careful not to bend the corners or get the paper crumpled.

The answer sheet normally has five vertical columns of numbers, with 30 numbers to a column. These numbers correspond to the question numbers in your test booklet. After each number, going across the page, are four or five pairs of dotted lines. These short dotted lines have small letters or numbers above them. The first two pairs may also have a "T" and "F" above the letters. This indicates that the first two pairs only are to be used if the questions are of the true-false type. If the questions are multiple-choice, disregard this "T" and "F" completely, and pay attention only to the small number or letters.

Answer your questions in the manner of the sample that follows. Proceed in the sequential steps outlined below.

Assume that you are answering question 32, which is:

32. The largest city in the United States is:
    A. Washington, D.C.   B. New York City   C. Chicago
    D. Detroit   E. San Francisco

1. Choose the answer you think is best.
    New York City is the largest, so choice B is correct.
2. Find the row of dotted lines numbered the same as the question you are answering.
    This is question number 32, so find row number 32.
3. Find the pair of dotted lines corresponding to the answer you have chosen.
    You have chosen answer B, so find the pair of dotted lines marked "B".
4. Make a solid black mark between the dotted lines.
    Go up and down two or three times with your pencil so plenty of graphite rubs off, but do not let the mark get outside or above the dots.

	T/A	F/B	C	D	E
29	::	::	::	::	::
30	A ::	B ::	C ::	D ::	E ::
31	A ::	B ::	C ::	D ::	E ::
32	A ::	B ▓	C ::	D ::	E ::
33	A ::	B ::	C ::	D ::	E ::

VI. BEFORE THE TEST

Common sense will help you find procedures to follow to get ready for an examination. Too many of us, however, overlook these sensible measures. Indeed, nervousness and fatigue have been found to be the most serious reasons why applicants fail to do their best on civil service tests. Here is a list of reminders.

1. Begin Your Preparation Early

   Don't wait until the last minute to go scurrying around for books and materials or to find out what the position is all about.

2. Prepare Continuously

   An hour a night for a week is better than an all-night cram session. This has been definitely established. What is more, a night a week for a month will return better dividends than crowding your study into a shorter period of time.

3. Locate the Place of the Examination

   You have been sent a notice telling you when and where to report for the examination. If the location is in a different town or otherwise unfamiliar to you, it would be well to inquire the best route and learn something about the building.

4. Relax the Night Before the Test

   Allow your mind to rest. Do not study at all that night. Plan some mild recreation or diversion; then go to bed early and get a good night's sleep.

5. Get Up Early Enough to Make a Leisurely Trip to the Place for the Test

   Then unforeseen events, traffic snarls, unfamiliar buildings, will not upset you.

6. Dress Comfortably

   A written test is not a fashion show. You will be known by number and not by name, so wear something comfortable.

7. Leave Excess Paraphernalia at Home

   Shopping bags and odd bundles will get in your way. You need bring only the items mentioned in the official notice sent to you; usually everything you need is provided. Do not bring reference books to the examination. They will only confuse those last minutes and be taken away from you when in the test room.

8. Arrive Somewhat Ahead of Time

   If because of transportation schedules you must get there very early, bring a newspaper or magazine to take your mind off yourself while waiting.

9. Locate the Examination Room

   When you have found the proper room, you will be directed to the seat or part of the room where you will sit. Sometimes you are given a sheet of instructions to read while you are waiting. Do not fill out any forms until you are told to do so; just read them and be ready.

10. Relax and Prepare to Listen to the Instructions

11. If you have any physical problem that may keep you from doing your best, be sure to tell the test administrator. If you are sick, or in poor health, you really cannot do your best on the test. You can come back and take the test some other time.

VII. AT THE TEST

   The day of the test is here and you have the test booklet in your hand. The temptation to get going is very strong. Caution! There is more to success than knowing the right answers. You must know how to identify your papers and understand variations in the type of short-answer question used in this particular examination. Follow these suggestions for maximum results from your efforts:

1. Cooperate with the Monitor

The test administrator has a duty to create a situation in which you can be as much at ease as possible. He will give instructions, tell you when to begin, check to see that you are marking your answer sheet correctly. He is not there to guard you, although he will see that your competitors do not take unfair advantage. He wants to help you do your best.

2. Listen to All Instructions

Don't jump the gun! Wait until you understand all directions. In most civil service tests you get more time than you need to answer the questions. So don't get in a hurry. Read each word of instructions until you clearly understand the meaning. Study the examples. Listen to all announcements. Follow directions. Ask questions if you do not understand what to do.

3. Identify Your Papers

Civil service examinations are usually identified by number only. You will be assigned a number; you must not put your name on your test papers. Be sure to copy your number correctly. Since more than one examination may be given, copy your exact examination title.

4. Plan Your Time

Unless you are told that a test is a "speed" or "rate-of-work" test, speed itself is not usually important. Time enough to answer all the questions will be provided. But this does not mean that you have all day. An overall time limit has been set. Divide the total time (in minutes) by the number of questions to get the approximate time you have for each question.

5. Do Not Linger Over Difficult Questions

If you come across a difficult question, mark it with a paper clip (useful to have along) and come back to it when you have been through the booklet. One caution if you do this -- be sure to skip a number on your answer sheet too. Check often to be sure that you have not lost your place and that you are marking in the row numbered the same as the question you are answering.

6. Read the Questions

Be sure you know what the question asks! Many capable people are unsuccessful because they failed to *read* the questions correctly.

7. Answer All Questions

Unless you have been instructed that a penalty will be deducted for incorrect answers, it is better to guess than to omit a question.

8. Speed Tests

It is often better *not* to guess on speed tests. It has been found that on timed tests people are tempted to spend the last few seconds before time is called in marking answers at random -- without even reading them -- in the hope of picking up a few extra points. To discourage this practice, the instructions may warn you that your score will be "corrected" for guessing. That is, a penalty will be applied. The incorrect answers will be deducted from the correct ones, or some other penalty formula will be used.

9. Review Your Answers

If you finish before time is called, go back to the questions you guessed or omitted to give further thought to them. Review other answers if you have time.

10. Return Your Test Materials

　　If you are ready to leave before others have finished or time is called, take *all* your materials to the monitor and leave quietly. Never take any test material with you. The monitor can discover whose papers are not complete, and taking a test booklet may be grounds for disqualification.

III. EXAMINATION TECHNIQUES

　　1. Read the *general* instructions carefully. These are usually printed on the first page of the examination booklet. As a rule, these instructions refer to the timing of the examination; the fact that you should not start work until the signal and must stop work at a signal, etc. If there are any *special* instructions, such as a choice of questions to be answered, make sure that you note this instruction carefully.

　　2. When you are ready to start work on the examination, that is as soon as the signal has been given, read the instructions to each question booklet, underline any key words or phrases, such as *least, best, outline, describe,* and the like. In this way you will tend to answer as requested rather than discover on reviewing your paper that you *listed without describing,* that you selected the *worst* choice rather than the *best* choice, etc.

　　3. If the examination is of the objective or so-called multiple-choice type, that is, each question will also give a series of possible answers: A, B, C, or D, and you are called upon to select the best answer and write the letter next to that answer on your answer paper, it is advisable to start answering each question in turn. There may be anywhere from 50 to 100 such questions in the three or four hours allotted and you can see how much time would be taken if you read through all the questions before beginning to answer any. Furthermore, if you come across a question or a group of questions which you know would be difficult to answer, it would undoubtedly affect your handling of all the other questions.

　　4. If the examination is of the esssay-type and contains but a few questions, it is a moot point as to whether you should read all the questions before starting to answer any one. Of course if you are given a choice, say five out of seven and the like, then it is essential to read all the questions so you can eliminate the two which are most difficult. If, however, you are asked to answer all the questions, there may be danger in trying to answer the easiest one first because you may find that you will spend too much time on it. The best technique is to answer the first question, then proceed to the second, etc.

　　5. Time your answers. Before the examination begins, write down the time it started, then add the time allowed for the examination and write down the time it must be completed, then divide the time available somewhat as follows:

　　(a) If $3\frac{1}{2}$ hours are allowed, that would be 210 minutes. If you have 80 objective-type questions, that would be an average of $2\frac{1}{2}$ minutes per question. Allow yourself no more than 2 minutes per question, or a total of 160 minutes, which will permit about 50 minutes to review.

　　(b) If for the time allotment of 210 minutes, there are 7 essay questions to answer, that would average about 30 minutes a question. Give yourself only 25 minutes per question so that you have about 35 minutes to review.

6. The most important instruction is *to read each question* and make sure you know what is wanted. The second most important instruction is to *time yourself properly* so that you answer every question. The third most important instruction is to *answer every question*. Guess if you have to but include something for each question. Remember that you will receive no credit for a blank and will probably receive some credit if you write something in answer to an essay question. If you guess a letter, say "B" for a multiple-choice question, you may have guessed right. If you leave a blank as the answer to a multiple-choice question, the examiners may respect your feelings but it will not add a point to your score.

7. Suggestions

  a. <u>Objective-Type Questions</u>

    (1) Examine the question booklet for proper sequence of pages and questions.

    (2) Read all instructions carefully.

    (3) Skip any question which seems too difficult; return to it after all other questions have been answered.

    (4) Apportion your time properly; do not spend too much time on any single question or group of questions.

    (5) Note and underline key words -- *all, most, fewest, least, best, worst, same, opposite.*

    (6) Pay particular attention to negatives.

    (7) Note unusual option, e.g., unduly long, short, complex, different or similar in content to the body of the question.

    (8) Observe the use of "hedging" words -- *probably, may, most likely, etc.*

    (9) Make sure that your answer is put next to the same number as the question.

    (10) Do not second-guess unless you have good reason to believe the second answer is definitely more correct.

    (11) Cross out original answer if you decide another answer is more accurate; do not erase.

    (12) Answer all questions; guess unless instructed otherwise.

    (13) Leave time for review.

  b. <u>Essay-Type Questions</u>

    (1) Read each question carefully.

    (2) Determine exactly what is wanted. Underline key words or phrases.

    (3) Decide on outline or paragraph answer.

    (4) Include many different points and elements unless asked to develop any one or two points or elements.

    (5) Show impartiality by giving pros and cons unless directed to select one side only.

    (6) Make and write down any assumptions you find necessary to answer the question.

    (7) Watch your English, grammar, punctuation, choice of words.

    (8) Time your answers; don't crowd material.

8. Answering the Essay Question

Most essay questions can be answered by framing the specific response around several key words or ideas. Here are a few such key words or ideas:

M's: manpower, materials, methods, money, management;
P's: purpose, program, policy, plan, procedure, practice, problems, pitfalls, personnel, public relations.

  a. <u>Six Basic Steps in Handling Problems</u>:
    (1) Preliminary plan and background development
    (2) Collect information, data and facts
    (3) Analyze and interpret information, data and facts
    (4) Analyze and develop solutions as well as make recommendations
    (5) Prepare report and sell recommendations
    (6) Install recommendations and follow up effectiveness

  b. <u>Pitfalls to Avoid</u>
    (1) *Taking things for granted*
       A statement of the situation does not necessarily imply that each of the elements is necessarily true; for example, a complaint may be invalid and biased so that all that can be taken for granted is that a complaint has been registered.
    (2) *Considering only one side of a situation*
       Wherever possible, indicate several alternatives and then point out the reasons you selected the best one.
    (3) *Failing to indicate follow-up*
       Whenever your answer indicates action on your part, make certain that you will take proper follow-up action to see how successful your recommendations, procedures, or actions turn out to be.
    (4) *Taking too long in answering any single question*
       Remember to time your answers properly.

IX. AFTER THE TEST

Scoring procedures differ in detail among civil service jurisdictions although the general principles are the same. Whether the papers are hand-scored or graded by the electric scoring machine we have described, they are nearly always graded by number. That is, the person who marks the paper knows only the number -- never the name -- of the applicant. Not until all the papers have been graded will they be matched with names. If other tests, such as training and experience or oral interview ratings have been given, scores will be combined. Different parts of the examination usually have different weights. For example, the written test might count 60 percent of the final grade, and a rating of training and experience 40 percent. In many jurisdictions, veterans will have a certain number of points added to their grades.

After the final grade has been determined, the names are placed in grade order and an eligible list is established. There are various methods for resolving ties between those who get the same final grade: probably the most common is to place first the name of the person whose application was received first. Job offers are made from the eligible list in the order the names appear on it.

You will be notified of your grade and your rank order as soon as all these computations have been made. This will be done as rapidly as possible.

People who are found to meet the requirements in the announcement are called "eligibles." Their names are put on a list of eligibles. An eligible's chances of getting a job depend on how high he stands on this list and how fast agencies are filling jobs from the list.

When a job is to be filled from a list of eligibles, the agency asks for the names of people on the list of eligibles for that job.

When the civil service commission receives this request, it sends to the agency the names of the three people highest on the list. Or, if the job to be filled has specialized requirements, the office sends the agency, from the general list, the names of the top three persons who meet those requirements.

The appointing officer makes a choice from among the three people whose names were sent to him. If the selected person accepts the appointment, the names of the others are put back on the list to be considered for future openings.

That is the rule in hiring from all kinds of eligible lists, whether they are for typist, carpenter, chemist, or something else. For every vacancy, the appointing officer has his choice of any one of the top three eligibles on the list. This explains why the person whose name is on top of the list sometimes does not get an appointment when some of the persons lower on the list do. If the appointing officer chooses the No.2 or No.3 eligible, the No.1 eligible does not get a job at once, but stays on the list until he is appointed or the list is terminated.

X. HOW TO PASS THE INTERVIEW TEST

The examination for which you applied requires an oral interview test. You have already taken the written test and you are now being called for the interview test -- the final part of the formal examination.

You may think that it is not possible to prepare for an interview test and that there are no procedures to follow during an interview.

Our purpose is to point out some things you can do in advance that will help you and some good rules to follow and pitfalls to avoid while you are being interviewed.

A. *WHAT IS AN INTERVIEW SUPPOSED TO TEST?*

The written examination is designed to test the technical knowledge and competence of the candidate; the oral is designed to evaluate intangible qualities, not readily measured otherwise, and to establish a list showing the relative fitness of each candidate, *as measured against his competitors,* for the position sought. Scoring is not on the basis of "right" or "wrong," but on a sliding scale of values ranging from "not passable" to "outstanding." As a matter of fact, it is possible to achieve a relatively low score without a single "incorrect" answer because of evident weakness in the qualities being measured,

Occasionally, an examination may consist entirely of an oral test -- either an individual or a group oral. In such cases, information is sought concerning the technical knowledges and abilities of the candidate, since there has been no written examination for this purpose. More commonly, however, an oral test is used to supplement a written examination.

B. *WHO CONDUCTS INTERVIEWS?*

The composition of oral boards varies among different jurisdictions. In nearly all, a representative of the personnel department serves as chairman. One of the members of the board may be a representative of the department in which the candidate would work. In some cases, "outside experts" are used, and, frequently, a business man or some other representative of the general public is asked to serve. Labor and management or other special groups may be represented. The aim is to secure the services of experts in the appropriate field.

However the board is composed, it is a good idea (and not at all improper or unethical) to ascertain in advance of the interview who the members are and what groups they represent. When you are introduced to them, you will have some idea of their backgrounds and interests, and at least you will not stutter and stammer over their names.

C. *WHAT TO DO BEFORE THE INTERVIEW*

While knowledge about the board members is useful and takes some of the surprise element out of the interview, there is other preparation which is more substantive. It *is* possible to prepare for an oral -- in several ways:

1. Keep a Copy of Your Application and Review it Carefully Before the Interview
   This may be the only document before the oral board, and the starting point of the interview. Know what experience and education you have listed there, and the sequence and dates of it. Sometimes the board will ask *you* to review the highlights of your experience for them; you should not have to hem and haw doing it.

2. Study the Class Specification and the Examination Announcement
   Usually, the oral board has one or both of these to guide them. The qualities, characteristics, or knowledges required by the position sought are stated in these documents. They offer valuable clues as to the nature of the oral interview. For example, if the job involves supervisory responsibilities, the announcement will usually indicate that knowledge of modern supervisory methods and the qualifications of the candidate as a supervisor will be tested. If so, you can expect such questions, frequently in the form of a hypothetical situation which you are expected to solve. *Never* go into an oral without knowledge of the duties and responsibilities of the job you seek.

3. Think Through Each Qualification Required
   Try to visualize the kind of questions *you* would ask if you were a board member. How well could you answer them? Try especially to appraise your own knowledge and background in each area, *measured against the job sought,* and identify any areas in which you are weak. Be critical and realistic -- do not flatter yourself.

4. Do Some General Reading in Areas in Which You Feel You May be Weak
   For example, if the job involves supervision and your past experience has *not,* some general reading in supervisory methods and practices, particularly in the field of human relations, might be useful. *Do not* study agency procedures or detailed manuals. The oral board will be testing your understanding and capacity, *not* your memory.

5. Get a Good Night's Sleep and Watch Your General Health and Mental Attitude
   You will want a clear head at the interview. Take care of a cold or other minor ailment, and, of course, *no hangovers.*

D. *WHAT TO DO THE DAY OF THE INTERVIEW*

Now comes the day of the interview itself. Give yourself plenty of time to get there. Plan to arrive somewhat ahead of the scheduled time, particularly if your appointment is in the fore part of the day. If a previous candidate fails to appear, the board might be ready for you a bit early. By early afternoon an oral board is almost invariably behind schedule if there are many candidates, and you may have to wait. Take along a book or magazine to read, or your application to review. But leave any extraneous material in the waiting room when you go in for your interview. In any event, relax and compose yourself.

The matter of dress is important. The board is forming impressions about you -- from your experience, your manners, your attitudes, and from your appearance. Give your personal appearance careful attention. Dress your *best*, but not your flashiest. Choose conservative, appropriate clothing, and be sure it and you are immaculate. This is a business interview, and your appearance should indicate that you regard it as such. Besides, being well-groomed and properly dressed will help boost your confidence.

Sooner or later, someone will call your name and escort you into the interview room. *This is it.* From here on you are on your own. It is too late for any more preparation. But, remember, you asked for this opportunity to prove your fitness, and you are here because your request was granted.

E. *WHAT HAPPENS WHEN YOU GO IN?*

The usual sequence of events will be as follows: The clerk (who is often the board stenographer) will introduce you to the chairman of the oral board, who will introduce you to each other member of the board. Acknowledge the introductions before you sit down. Do not be surprised if you find a microphone facing you or a stenotypist sitting by. Oral interviews are usually recorded, in the event of an appeal or other review.

Usually the chairman of the board will open the interview by reviewing the highlights of your education and work experience from your application -- primarily for the benefit of the other members of the board, as well as to get the material into the record. Do not interrupt or comment unless there is an error or significant misinterpretation; if so, do not hesitate. But do not quibble about insignificant matters. Usually, also, he will ask you some question about your education, your experience, or your present job -- partly to get you started talking, to establish the interviewing "rapport." He may start the actual questioning, or turn it over to one of the other members. Frequently each member undertakes the questioning on a particular area, one in which he is perhaps most competent. So you can expect each member to participate in the examination. And because the time is limited, you may expect some rather abrupt switches in the direction the questioning takes. Do not be upset by it. Normally, a board member will not pursue a single line of questioning unless he discovers a particular strength or weakness.

After each member has participated, the chairman will usually ask whether any member has any further questions, then will ask you if you have anything you wish to add. Unless you are expecting this question, it may floor you. Or worse, it may start you off on an extended, extemporaneous speech. The board is not usually seeking more information. The question is principally to offer you a last opportunity to present further qualifications or to indicate that you have nothing to add. So, if you feel that a significant qualification or characteristic has been overlooked, it is proper to point it out in a sentence or so. Do not compliment the board on the thoroughness of their examination -- they have been sketchy, and you know it. If you wish, merely say, "No thank you, I have nothing further to add." This is a point where you can "talk yourself out" of a good impression or fail to present an important bit of information. *Remember, you close the interview yourself.*

The chairman will then say,"That is all,Mr.Smith,thank you." Do not be startled; the interview is over, and quicker than you think. Say,"Thank you and good morning," gather up your belongings and take your leave. Save your sigh of relief for the other side of the door.

F. *HOW TO PUT YOUR BEST FOOT FORWARD*

Throughout all this process, you may feel that the board individually and collectively is trying to pierce your defenses, to seek out your hidden weaknesses, and to embarrass and confuse you. Actually, this is not true. They are obliged to make an appraisal of your qualifications for the job you are seeking, and they *want to see you in your best light*. Remember, they must interview all candidates and a noncooperative candidate may become a failure in spite of their best efforts to bring out his qualifications. Here are fifteen(15) suggestions that will help you:

1. Be Natural. Keep Your Attitude Confident,But Not Cocky

If *you* are not confident that you can do the job, do not expect the *board* to be. Do not apologize for your weaknesses, try to bring out your strong points. The board is interested in a positive, not a negative presentation. Cockiness will antagonize any board member, and make him wonder if you are covering up a weakness by a false show of strength.

2. Get Comfortable, But Don't Lounge or Sprawl

Sit erectly but not stiffly. A careless posture may lead the board to conclude you are careless in other things, or at least that you are not impressed by the importance of the occasion to you.Either conclusion is natural, even if incorrect. Do not fuss with your clothing, or with a pencil or an ashtray. Your hands may occasionally be useful to emphasize a point; do not let them become a point of distraction.

3. Do Not Wisecrack or Make Small Talk

This is a serious situation, and your attitude should show that you consider it as such. Further, the time of the board is limited; they do not want to waste it, and neither should you.

4. Do Not Exaggerate Your Experience or Abilities

In the first place, from information in the application,from other interviews and other sources, the board may know more about you than you think; in the second place, you probably will not get away with it in the first place. An experienced board is rather adept at spotting such a situation. Do not take the chance.

5. If You Know a Member of the Board, Do Not Make a Point of It, Yet Do Not Hide It.

Certainly you are not fooling him, and probably not the other members of the board. Do not try to take advantage of your acquaintanceship -- it will probably do you little good.

6. Do Not Dominate the Interview

Let the board do that. They will give you the clues -- do not assume that you have to do all the talking. Realize that the board has a number of questions to ask you, and do not try to take up all the interview time by showing off your extensive knowledge of the answer to the first one.

7. Be Attentive

You only have twenty minutes or so, and you should keep your attention at its sharpest throughout. When a member is addressing a problem or a question to you, give him your undivided attention. Address your reply principally to him, but do not exclude the other members of the board.

8. Do Not Interrupt

A board member may be stating a problem for you to analyze. He will ask you a question when the time comes. Let him state the problem, and wait for the question.

9. Make Sure You Understand the Question

Do not try to answer until you are sure what the question is. If it is not clear, restate it in your own words or ask the board member to clarify it for you. But do not haggle about minor elements.

10. Reply Promptly But Not Hastily

A common entry on oral board rating sheets is "candidate responded readily," or "candidate hesitated in replies." Respond as promptly and quickly as you can, but do not jump to a hasty, ill-considered answer.

11. Do Not Be Peremptory in Your Answers

A brief answer is proper -- but do not fire your answer back. That is a losing game from your point of view. The board member can probably ask questions much faster than you can answer them.

12. Do Not Try To Create the Answer You Think the Board Member Wants

He is interested in what kind of · mind you have and how it works -- not in playing games. Furthermore, he can usually spot this practice and will usually grade you down on it.

13. Do Not Switch Sides in Your Reply Merely to Agree With a Board Member

Frequently, a member will take a contrary position merely to draw you out and to see if you are willing and able to defend your point of view. Do not start a debate, yet do not surrender a good position. If a position is worth taking, it is worth defending.

14. Do Not Be Afraid to Admit an Error in Judgment if You Are Shown to Be Wrong

The board knows that you are forced to reply without any opportunity for careful consideration. Your answer may be demonstrably wrong. If so, admit it and get on with the interview.

15. Do Not Dwell at Length on Your Present Job

The opening question may relate to your present assignment. Answer the question but do not go into an extended discussion. You are being examined for a *new* job, not your present one. As a matter of fact, try to phrase *all* your answers in terms of the job for which you are being examined.

G. BASIS OF RATING

Probably you will forget most of these "do's" and "don'ts" when you walk into the oral interview room. Even remembering them all will not insure you a passing grade. Perhaps you did not have the qualifications in the first place. But remembering them *will* help you to put your best foot forward, without treading on the toes of the board members.

Rumor and popular opinion to the contrary notwithstanding, an oral board wants you to make the best appearance possible. They know you are under pressure -- but they also want to see how you respond to it as a guide to what your reaction would be under the pressures of the job you seek. They will be influenced by the degree of poise you display, the personal traits you show, and the manner in which you respond.

EXAMINATION SECTION

EXAMINATION SECTION

DIRECTIONS: Each question or incomplete statement is followed by several suggested answers or completions. Select the one that BEST answers the question or completes the statement. *PRINT THE LETTER OF THE CORRECT ANSWER IN THE SPACE AT THE RIGHT.*

Questions 1-5.

TEST 1

DIRECTIONS: Questions 1 through 5 are to be answered on the basis of the extracts from Federal income tax withholding and social security tax tables shown below. These tables indicate the amounts which must be withheld from the employee's salary by his employer for Federal income tax and for social security. They are based on weekly earnings.

INCOME TAX WITHHOLDING TABLE						
The wages are		And the number of withholding allowances is				
At least	But less than	5	6	7	8	9	10 or more
		The amount of income tax to be withheld shall be				
$150	$160	$12.30	$ 9.50	$ 6.90	$ 4.30	$ 2.00	$ 0
160	170	14.40	11.40	8.70	6.10	3.50	1.40
170	180	16.50	13.50	10.50	7.90	5.30	2.80
180	190	18.60	15.60	12.60	9.70	7.10	4.50
190	200	20.70	17.70	14.70	11.70	8.90	6.30
200	210	22.80	19.80	16.80	13.80	10.70	8.10
210	220	24.90	21.90	18.90	15.90	12.80	9.90
220	230	27.00	24.00	21.00	18.00	14.90	11.90
230	240	29.10	26.10	23.10	20.10	17.00	14.00
240	250	31.20	28.20	25.20	22.20	19.10	16.10

SOCIAL SECURITY TABLE					
WAGES		Tax to be withheld	WAGES		Tax to be withheld
At least	But less than		At least	But less than	
$166.59	$166.76	$9.75	$168.30	$168.47	$9.85
166.76	166.93	9.76	168.47	168.64	9.86
166.93	167.10	9.77	168.64	168.81	9.87
167.10	167.27	9.78	168.81	168.98	9.88
167.27	167.44	9.79	168.98	169.15	9.89
167.44	167.61	9.80	169.15	169.32	9.90
167.61	167.78	9.81	169.32	169.49	9.91
167.78	167.95	9.82	169.49	169.66	9.92
167.95	168.12	9.83	169.66	169.83	9.93
168.12	168.30	9.84	169.83	170.00	9.94

1. If an employee has a weekly wage of $189.75 and claims
   6 withholding allowances, the amount of income tax to be
   withheld is
      A. $13.50   B. $15.60   C. $17.70   D. $18.60   1.___

2. An employee had wages of $167.80 for one week.
   With eight withholding allowances claimed, how much income
   tax will be withheld from his salary?
      A. $4.30   B. $6.10   C. $6.90   D. $8.70   2.___

3. How much social security tax will an employee with weekly
   wages of $167.80 pay?
      A. $9.80   B. $9.81   C. $9.82   D. $9.83   3.___

4. Mr. Wise earns $169.90 a week and claims seven withholding
   allowances.
   What is his take-home pay after income tax and social
   security tax are deducted?
      A. $150.16   B. $151.26   C. $159.96   D. $161.20   4.___

5. If an employee pays $9.87 in social security tax and
   claims eight withholding allowances, the amount of income
   tax that should be withheld from his wages is
      A. $4.30   B. $6.10   C. $6.90   D. $7.90   5.___

6. A fundamental rule of bookkeeping states that an individual's assets equal his liabilities plus his proprietorship (ASSETS = LIABILITIES + PROPRIETORSHIP).
   Which of the following statements logically follows from
   this rule?
      A. ASSETS = PROPRIETORSHIP - LIABILITIES
      B. LIABILITIES = ASSETS + PROPRIETORSHIP
      C. PROPRIETORSHIP = ASSETS - LIABILITIES
      D. PROPRIETORSHIP = LIABILITIES + ASSETS   6.___

7. Mr. Martin's assets consist of the following: 7.___
         Cash on hand: $5,233.74
         Furniture: $4,925.00
         Government Bonds: $5,500.00
   What are his TOTAL assets?
      A. $10,158.74   B. $10,425.00
      C. $10,733.74   D. $15,658.74

8. If Mr. Mitchell has $627.04 in his checking account and   8.___
   then writes three checks for $241.75, $13.24, and $102.97,
   what will be his new balance?
      A. $257.88   B. $269.08   C. $357.96   D. $369.96

9. An employee's net pay is equal to his total earnings less   9.___
   all deductions.
   If an employee's total earnings in a pay period are $497.05,
   what is his NET pay if he has the following deductions:
   Federal income tax, $90.32; FICA, $28.74; State tax,
   $18.79; City tax, $7.25; Pension, $1.88?
      A. $351.17   B. $351.07   C. $350.17   D. $350.07

10. A petty cash fund had an opening balance of $85.75 on   10.___
    December 1. Expenditures of $23.00, $15.65, $5.23, $14.75,
    and $26.38 were made out of this fund during the first 14
    days of the month. Then, on December 17, another $38.50
    was added to the fund.
    If additional expenditures of $17.18, $3.29, and $11.64
    were made during the remainder of the month, what was the
    FINAL balance of the petty cash fund at the end of
    December?
    A. $6.93   B. $7.13   C. $46.51   D. $91.40

Questions 11-15.

DIRECTIONS: Questions 11 through 15 are to be answered on the basis
              of the following instructions.

    The chart below is used by the loan division of a city retirement
system for the following purposes: (1) to calculate the monthly
payment a member must pay on an outstanding loan; (2) to calculate
how much a member owes on an outstanding loan after he has made a
number of payments.

    To calculate the amount a member must pay each month in repaying
his loan, look at Column II on the chart. You will notice that each
entry in Column II corresponds to a number appearing under the *Months*
column; for example, 1.004868 corresponds to 1 month, 0.503654 corresponds to 2 months, etc. To calculate the amount a member must pay
each month, use the following procedure: multiply the amount of the
loan by the entry in Column II which corresponds to the number of
months over which the loan will be paid back. For example, if a loan
of $200 is taken out for six months, multiply $200 by 0.169518, the
entry in Column II which corresponds to six months.

    In order to calculate the balance still owed on an outstanding
loan, multiply the monthly payment by the number in Column I which
corresponds to the number of monthly payments which remain to be
paid on the loan. For example, if a member is supposed to pay
$106.00 a month for twelve months, after seven payments, five monthly
payments remain. To calculate the balance owed on the loan at this
point, multiply the $106.00 monthly payment by 4.927807, the number
in Column I that corresponds to five months.

Months	Column I	Column II
1	0.995156	1.004868
2	1.985491	0.503654
3	2.971029	0.336584
4	3.951793	0.253050
5	4.927807	0.202930
6	5.899092	0.169518
7	6.865673	0.145652
8	7.827572	0.127754
9	8.784811	0.113833
10	9.737414	0.102697
11	10.685402	0.093586
12	11.628798	0.085993
13	12.567624	0.079570
14	13.501902	0.074064
15	14.431655	0.069292

11. If Mr. Carson borrows $1,500 for eight months, how much   11.___
    will he have to pay back each month?
        A. $187.16   B. $191.63   C. $208.72   D. $218.65

12. If a member borrows $2,400 for one year, the amount he   12.___
    will have to pay back each month is
        A. $118.78   B. $196.18   C. $202.28   D. $206.38

13. Mr. Elliott borrowed $1,700 for a period of fifteen   13.___
    months.
    Each month he will have to pay back
        A. $117.80   B. $116.96   C. $107.79   D. $101.79

14. Mr. Aylward is paying back a thirteen-month loan at the   14.___
    rate of $173.13 a month.
    If he has already made six monthly payments, how much
    does he owe on the outstanding loan?
        A. $1,027.39 B. $1,178.75 C. $1,188.65 D. $1,898.85

15. A loan was taken out for 15 months, and the monthly   15.___
    payment was $104.75.
    After two monthly payments, how much was still owed on
    this loan?
        A. $515.79   B. $863.89   C. $1,116.76 D. $1,316.46

16. The ABC Corporation had a gross income of $125,500.00 in   16.___
    1988. Of this, it paid 60% for overhead.
    If the gross income for 1989 increased by $6,500 and the
    cost of overhead increased to 61% of gross income, how
    much more did it pay for overhead in 1989 than in 1988?
        A. $1,320   B. $5,220   C. $7,530   D. $8,052

17. After one year, Mr. Richards paid back a total of   17.___
    $1,695.00 as payment for a $1,500.00 loan. All the
    money paid over $1,500.00 was simple interest.
    The interest charge was MOST NEARLY
        A. 13%   B. 11%   C. 9%   D. 7%

18. A checking account has a balance of $253.36.   18.___
    If deposits of $36.95, $210.23, and $7.34 and withdrawals
    of $117.35, $23.37, and $15.98 are made, what is the NEW
    balance of the account?
        A. $155.54   B. $351.18   C. $364.58   D. $664.58

19. In 1988, the W Realty Company spent 27% of its income   19.___
    on rent.
    If it earned $97,254.00 in 1988, the amount it paid for
    rent was
        A. $26,258.58   B. $26,348.58
        C. $27,248.58   D. $27,358.58

20. Six percent simple annual interest on $2,436.18 is   20.___
    MOST NEARLY
        A. $145.08   B. $145.17   C. $146.08   D. $146.17

21. Assume that the XYZ Company has $10,402.72 cash on hand. If it pays $699.83 of this for rent, the amount of cash on hand would be
    A. $9,792.89   B. $9,702.89
    C. $9,692.89   D. $9,602.89

21.___

22. On January 31, Mr. Warren's checking account had a balance of $933.68.
    If he deposited $36.40 on February 2, $126.00 on February 9, and $90.02 on February 16, and wrote no checks during this period, what was the balance of his account on February 17?
    A. $680.26   B. $681.26   C. $1,186.10   D. $1,187.00

22.___

23. Multiplying a number by .75 is the same as
    A. *multiplying* it by 2/3   B. *dividing* it by 2/3
    C. *multiplying* it by 3/4   D. *dividing* it by 3/4

23.___

24. In City Agency A, 2/3 of the employees are enrolled in a retirement system. City Agency B has the same number of employees as Agency A, and 60% of these are enrolled in a retirement system.
    If Agency A has a total of 660 employees, how many MORE employees does it have enrolled in a retirement system than does Agency B?
    A. 36   B. 44   C. 56   D. 66

24.___

25. Net Worth is equal to Assets minus Liabilities.
    If, at the end of 1988, a textile company had assets of $98,695.83 and liabilities of $59,238.29, what was its net worth?
    A. $38,478.54   B. $38,488.64
    C. $39,457.54   D. $48,557.54

25.___

KEY (CORRECT ANSWERS)

1. B		11. B	
2. B		12. D	
3. C		13. A	
4. B		14. C	
5. B		15. D	
6. C		16. B	
7. D		17. A	
8. B		18. B	
9. D		19. A	
10. B		20. D	

21. B
22. C
23. C
24. B
25. C

TEST 2

DIRECTIONS: Each question or incomplete statement is followed by several suggested answers or completions. Select the one that BEST answers the question or completes the statement. *PRINT THE LETTER OF THE CORRECT ANSWER IN THE SPACE AT THE RIGHT.*

Questions 1-10.

DIRECTIONS: Questions 1 through 10 below present the identification numbers, initials, and last names of employees enrolled in a city personnel system. You are to choose the option (A, B, C, or D) that has the IDENTICAL identification number, initials, and last name as those given in each question.

<u>Sample Question</u>

    B145698 JL Jones
      A. B146798 JL Jones   B. B145698 JL Jonas
      C. P145698 JL Jones   D. B145698 JL Jones

The correct answer is D. Only Option D shows the identification number, initials, and last name exactly as they are in the sample question. Options A, B, and C have errors in the identification number or last name.

1. J297483 PL Robinson   1.____
   A. J294783 PL Robinson   B. J297483 PL Robinson
   C. J297483 PI Robinson   D. J297843 PL Robinson

2. S497662 JG Schwartz   2.____
   A. S497662 JG Schwarz   B. S497762 JG Schwartz
   C. S497662 JG Schwartz   D. S497663 JG Schwartz

3. G696436 LN Alberton   3.____
   A. G696436 LM Alberton   B. G696436 LN Albertson
   C. G696346 LN Albertson   D. G696436 LN Alberton

4. R774923 AD Aldrich   4.____
   A. R774923 AD Aldrich   B. R744923 AD Aldrich
   C. R774932 AP Aldrich   D. R774932 AD Allrich

5. N239638 RP Hrynyk   5.____
   A. N236938 PR Hrynyk   B. N236938 RP Hrynyk
   C. N239638 PR Hrynyk   D. N239638 RP Hrynyk

6. R156949 LT Carlson   6.____
   A. R156949 LT Carlton   B. R156494 LT Carlson
   C. R159649 LT Carlton   D. R156949 LT Carlson

7. T524697 MN Orenstein   7.___
    A. T524697 MN Orenstein   B. T524967 MN Orinstein
    C. T524697 NM Ornstein   D. T524967 NM Orenstein

8. L346239 JD Remsen   8.___
    A. L346239 JD Remson   B. L364239 JD Remsen
    C. L346329 JD Remsen   D. L346239 JD Remsen

9. P966438 SB Rieperson   9.___
    A. P996438 SB Reiperson   B. P966438 SB Reiperson
    C. R996438 SB Rieperson   D. P966438 SB Rieperson

10. D749382 CD Thompson   10.___
    A. P749382 CD Thompson   B. D749832 CD Thomsonn
    C. D749382 CD Thompson   D. D749823 CD Thomspon

Questions 11-20.

DIRECTIONS: Assume that each of the capital letters in the table
below represents the name of an employee enrolled in
the city's employees' personnel system. The number
directly beneath the letter represents the agency
for which the employee works, and the small letter
directly beneath represents the code for the employee's
account.

Name of Employee	L	O	T	Q	A	M	R	N	C
Agency	3	4	5	9	8	7	2	1	6
Account Code	r	f	b	i	d	t	g	e	n

In each of the following Questions 11 through 20, the
agency code numbers and the account code letters in
Columns 2 and 3 should correspond to the capital letters
in Column 1 and should be in the same consecutive order.
For each question, look at each column carefully and
mark your answer as follows:

If there are one or more errors in Column 2 *only*, mark
your answer A.
If there are one or more errors in Column 3 *only*, mark
your answer B.
If there are one or more errors in Column 2 and one or
more errors in Column 3, mark your answer C.
If there are NO errors in either column, mark your
answer D.

SAMPLE QUESTION

Column 1	Column 2	Column 3
T Q L M O C	5 8 3 7 4 6	b i r t f n

In Column 2, the second agency code number (corresponding
to letter Q) should be 9, not 8. Column 3 is coded
correctly to Column 1. Since there is an error only in
Column 2, the correct answer is A.

COLUMN 1	COLUMN 2	COLUMN 3	
11. Q L N R C A	9 3 1 2 6 8	i r e g n d	11. ___
12. N R M O T C	1 2 7 5 4 6	e g f t b n	12. ___
13. R C T A L M	2 6 5 8 3 7	g n d b r t	13. ___
14. T A M L O N	5 7 8 3 4 1	b d t r f e	14. ___
15. A N T O R M	8 1 5 4 2 7	d e b i g t	15. ___
16. M R A L O N	7 2 8 3 4 1	t g d r f e	16. ___
17. C T N Q R O	6 5 7 9 2 4	n d e i g f	17. ___
18. Q M R O T A	9 7 2 4 5 8	i t g f b d	18. ___
19. R Q M C O L	2 9 7 4 6 3	g i t n f r	19. ___
20. N O M R T Q	1 4 7 2 5 9	e f t g b i	20. ___

Questions 21-25.

DIRECTIONS: Questions 21 through 25 are to be answered SOLELY on the basis of the following passage.

The city may issue its own bonds or it may purchase bonds as an investment. Bonds may be issued in various denominations, and the face value of the bond is its par value. Before purchasing a bond, the investor desires to know the rate of income that the investment will yield. In computing the yield on a bond, it is assumed that the investor will keep the bond until the date of maturity, except for callable bonds which are not considered in this passage. To compute exact yield is a complicated mathematical problem, and scientifically prepared tables are generally used to avoid such computation. However, the approximate yield can be computed much more easily. In computing approximate yield, the accrued interest on the date of purchase should be ignored because the buyer who pays accrued interest to the seller receives it again at the next interest date. Bonds bought at a premium (which cost more) yield a lower rate of income than the same bonds bought at par (face value), and bonds bought at a discount (which cost less) yield a higher rate of income than the same bonds bought at par.

21. An investor bought a $10,000 city bond paying 6% interest. 21. ___
Which of the following purchase prices would indicate that the bond was bought at a premium?
A. $9,000 B. $9,400 C. $10,000 D. $10,600

22. During 1988, a particular $10,000 bond paying 7½% sold 22. ___
at fluctuating prices.
Which of the following prices would indicate that the bond was bought at a discount?
A. $9,800 B. $10,000 C. $10,200 D. $10,750

23. A certain group of bonds was sold in denominations of   23.___
    $5,000, $10,000, $20,000, and $50,000.
    In the following list of four purchase prices, which
    one is MOST likely to represent a bond sold at par value?
       A. $10,500   B. $20,000   C. $22,000   D. $49,000

24. When computing the approximate yield on a bond, it is   24.___
    DESIRABLE to
       A. assume the bond was purchased at par
       B. consult scientifically prepared tables
       C. ignore accrued interest on the date of purchase
       D. wait until the bond reaches maturity

25. Which of the following is MOST likely to be an exception   25.___
    to the information provided in the above passage?
    Bonds
       A. purchased at a premium   B. sold at par
       C. sold before maturity   D. which are callable

KEY (CORRECT ANSWERS)

1. B		11. D	
2. C		12. C	
3. D		13. B	
4. A		14. A	
5. D		15. B	
6. D		16. D	
7. A		17. C	
8. D		18. D	
9. D		19. A	
10. C		20. D	

21. D
22. A
23. B
24. C
25. D

TEST 3

Questions 1-6.

DIRECTIONS: Questions 1 through 6 consist of computations of addition, subtraction, multiplication, and division. For each question, do the computation indicated, and choose the correct answer from the four choices given.

1. ADD: 8936
         7821
         8953
         4297
         9785
         6579

   A. 45371   B. 45381   C. 46371   D. 46381   1.____

2. SUBTRACT: 95,432
              67,596

   A. 27,836   B. 27,846   C. 27,936   D. 27,946   2.____

3. MULTIPLY: 987
              867

   A. 854609   B. 854729   C. 855709   D. 855729   3.____

4. DIVIDE: 59)321439.0

   A. 5438.1   B. 5447.1   C. 5448.1   D. 5457.1   4.____

5. DIVIDE: .057)721

   A. 12,648.0   B. 12,648.1   C. 12,649.0   D. 12,649.1   5.____

6. ADD: ½ + 5/7

   A. 1 3/14   B. 1 2/7   C. 1 5/14   D. 1 3/7   6.____

7. If the total number of employees in one city agency   7.___
    increased from 1,927 to 2,006 during a certain year,
    the percentage increase in the number of employees for
    that year is MOST NEARLY
        A. 4%   B. 5%   C. 6%   D. 7%

8. During a single fiscal year, which totaled 248 workdays, 8.___
    one account clerk verified 1,488 purchase vouchers.
    Assuming a normal work week of five days, what is the
    average number of vouchers verified by the account clerk
    in a one-week period during this fiscal year?
        A. 25   B. 30   C. 35   D. 40

9. If the city department of purchase bought 190 electric   9.___
    typewriters for $793.50 each and 208 electronic typewriters
    for $839.90 each, the TOTAL price paid for these
    typewriters is
        A. $315,813.00   B. $325,464.20
        C. $334,278.20   D. $335.863.00

Questions 10-14.

DIRECTIONS: Questions 10 through 14 are to be answered SOLELY on the
             basis of the information given in the following paragraph.

    Since discounts are in common use in the commercial world and
apply to purchases made by government agencies as well as business
firms, it is essential that individuals in both public and private
employment who prepare bills, check invoices, prepare payment vouchers,
or write checks to pay bills have an understanding of the terms used.
These include cash or time discount, trade discount, and discount
series. A cash or time discount offers a reduction in price to the
buyer for the prompt payment of the bill and is usually expressed as
a percentage with a time requirement, stated in days, within which
the bill must be paid in order to earn the discount. An example
would be 3/10, meaning a 3% discount may be applied to the bill if
the payment is forwarded to the vendor within ten days. On an
invoice, the cash discount terms are usually followed by the net terms,
which is the time in days allowed for ordinary payment of the bill.
Thus, 3/10, Net 30 means that full payment is expected in thirty days
if the cash discount of 3% is not taken for having paid the bill
within ten days. When the expression Terms Net Cash is listed on a
bill, it means that no deduction for early payment is allowed. A
trade discount is normally applied to list prices by a manufacturer
to show the actual price to retailers so that they may know their
cost and determine markups that will allow them to operate competi-
tively and at a profit. A trade discount is applied by the seller
to the list price and is independent of a cash or time discount.
Discounts may also be used by manufacturers to adjust prices charged
to retailers without changing list prices. This is usually done by
series discounting and is expressed as a series of percentages. To
compute a series discount, such as 40%, 20%, 10%, first apply the
40% discount to the list price, then apply the 20% discount to the
remainder, and finally apply the 10% discount to the second remainder.

10. According to the above passage, trade discounts are   10.___
    A. applied by the buyer
    B. independent of cash discounts
    C. restricted to cash sales
    D. used to secure rapid payment of bills

11. According to the above passage, if the sales terms 5/10,   11.___
    Net 60 appear on a bill in the amount of $100 dated
    December 5, 1988 and the buyer submits his payment on
    December 15, 1988, his PROPER payment should be
    A. $60   B. $90   C. $95   D. $100

12. According to the above passage, if a manufacturer gives a   12.___
    trade discount of 40% for an item with a list price of
    $250 and the terms are Net Cash, the price a retail
    merchant is required to pay for this item is
    A. $250   B. $210   C. $150   D. $100

13. According to the above passage, a series discount of 25%,   13.___
    20%, 10% applied to a list price of $200 results in an
    ACTUAL price to the buyer of
    A. $88   B. $90   C. $108   D. $110

14. According to the above passage, if a manufacturer gives   14.___
    a trade discount of 50% and the terms are 6/10, Net 30,
    the cost to a retail merchant of an item with a list price
    of $500 and for which he takes the time discount is
    A. $220   B. $235   C. $240   D. $250

Questions 15-22.

DIRECTIONS: Questions 15 through 22 each show in Column I the informa-
               tion written on five cards (lettered j, k, l, m, n) which
               have to be filed. You are to choose the option (lettered
               A, B, C, or D) in Column II which BEST represents the
               proper order of filing according to the information,
               rules, and sample question given below.

               A file card record is kept of the work assignments for
               all the employees in a certain bureau. On each card is
               the employee's name, the date of work assignment, and
               the work assignment code number. The cards are to be
               filed according to the following rules:

               FIRST: File in alphabetical order according to employee'
                         name.
               SECOND: When two or more cards have the same employee's
                         name, file according to the assignment date,
                         beginning with the earliest date.
               THIRD: When two or more cards have the same employee's
                         name and the same date, file according to the
                         work assignment number beginning with the lowest
                         number.

               Column II shows the cards arranged in four different order
               Pick the option (A, B, C, or D) in Column II which shows
               the correct arrangement of the cards according to the
               above filing rules.

SAMPLE QUESTION

Column I	Column II
(j) Cluney 4/8/82 (486503)	A. k, l, m, j, n
(k) Roster 5/10/81 (246611)	B. k, n, j, l, m
(l) Altool 10/15/82 (711433)	C. l, k, j, m, n
(m) Cluney 12/18/82 (527610)	D. l, n, j, m, k
(n) Cluney 4/8/82 (486500)	

The correct way to file the cards is:
```
(l) Altool  10/15/82 (711433)
(n) Cluney   4/8/82  (486500)
(j) Cluney   4/8/82  (486503)
(m) Cluney  12/18/82 (527610)
(k) Roster   5/10/81 (246611)
```

The correct filing order is shown by the letters l, n, j, m, k. The answer to the sample question is the letter D, which appears in front of the letters l, n, j, m, k in Column II.

COLUMN I   COLUMN II

15. (j) Smith   3/19/83 (662118)   A. j, m, l, n, k   15.___
     (k) Turner 4/16/79 (481349)   B. j, l, n, m, k
     (l) Terman 3/20/82 (210229)   C. k, n, m, l, j
     (m) Smyth   3/20/82 (481359)   D. j, n, k, l, m
     (n) Terry   5/11/81 (672128)

16. (j) Ross   5/29/82 (396118)   A. l, m, k, n, j   16.___
     (k) Rosner 5/29/82 (439281)   B. m, l, k, n, j
     (l) Rose   7/19/82 (723456)   C. l, m, k, j, n
     (m) Rosen   5/29/83 (829692)   D. m, l, j, n, k
     (n) Ross   5/29/82 (399118)

17. (j) Sherd   10/12/79 (552368) A. n, m, k, j, l   17.___
     (k) Snyder   11/12/79 (539286) B. j, m, l, k, n
     (l) Shindler 10/13/78 (426798) C. m, k, n, j, l
     (m) Scherld   10/12/79 (552386) D. m, n, j, l, k
     (n) Schneider 11/12/79 (798213)

18. (j) Carter 1/16/82 (489636)   A. k, n, j, l, m   18.___
     (k) Carson 2/16/81 (392671)   B. n, k, m, l, j
     (l) Carter 1/16/81 (486936)   C. n, k, l, j, m
     (m) Carton 3/15/80 (489639)   D. k, n, l, j, m
     (n) Carson 2/16/81 (392617)

19. (j) Thomas   3/18/79 (763182)   A. m, l, j, k, n   19.___
     (k) Tompkins 3/19/80 (928439)   B. j, m, l, k, n
     (l) Thomson 3/21/80 (763812)   C. j, l, n, m, k
     (m) Thompson 3/18/79 (924893)   D. l, m, j, n, k
     (n) Tompson 3/19/79 (928793)

COLUMN I | COLUMN II

20.
(j) Breit   8/10/83 (345612)
(k) Briet   5/21/80 (837543)
(l) Bright 9/18/79 (931827)
(m) Breit   3/7/78 (553984)
(n) Brent   6/14/84 (682731)

A. m, j, n, k, l
B. n, m, j, k, l
C. m, j, k, l, n
D. j, m, k, l, n

20.___

21.
(j) Roberts 10/19/82 (581932)
(k) Rogers 8/9/80 (638763)
(l) Rogerts 7/15/77 (105689)
(m) Robin   3/8/72 (287915)
(n) Rogers 4/2/84 (736921)

A. n, k, l, m, j
B. n, k, l, j, m
C. k, n, l, m, j
D. j, m, k, n, l

21.___

22.
(j) Hebert   4/28/82 (719468)
(k) Herbert 5/8/81 (938432)
(l) Helbert 9/23/84 (832912)
(m) Herbst   7/10/83 (648599)
(n) Herbert 5/8/81 (487627)

A. n, k, j, m, l
B. j, l, n, k, m
C. l, j, k, n, m
D. l, j, n, k, m

22.___

23. In order to pay its employees, the Convex Company obtained bills and coins in the following denominations:

Denomination	$20	$10	$5	$1	$.50	$.25	$.10	$.05	$.01
Number	317	122	38	73	69	47	39	25	36

What was the TOTAL amount of cash obtained?
A. $7,874.76   B. $7,878.00
C. $7,889.25   D. $7,924.35

23.___

24. H. Partridge receives a weekly gross salary (before deductions) of $198.75. Through weekly payroll deductions of $6.59, he is paying back a loan he took from his pension fund.
If other fixed weekly deductions amount to $61.38, how much pay would Mr. Partridge take home over a period of 33 weeks?
A. $3,815.64   B. $4,125.23
C. $4,315.74   D. $6,558.75

24.___

25. Mr. Robertson is a city employee enrolled in a city retirement system. He has taken out a loan from the retirement fund and is paying it back at the rate of $14.90 every two weeks.
In eighteen weeks, how much money will he have paid back on the loan?
A. $268.20   B. $152.80   C. $134.10   D. $67.05

25.___

26. In 1989, the Iridor Book Company had the following expenses: rent, $6,500; overhead, $52,585; inventory, $35,700; and miscellaneous, $1,275.
If all of these expenses went up 18% in 1990, what would they TOTAL in 1990?
A. $17,290.80   B. $78,769.20
C. $96,060.00   D. $113,350.80

26.___

27. Ms. Ranier had a gross salary of $355.36, paid once every week.
If the deductions from each paycheck are $62.72, $25.13, $6.29, and $1.27, how much money would Ms. Ranier take home in four weeks?
    A. $1,039.80   B. $1,421.44
    C. $2,079.60   D. $2,842.88

27.___

28. Mr. Martin had a net income of $19,100 for the year.
If he spent 34% on rent and household expenses, 3% on house furnishings, 25% on clothes, and 36% on food, how much was left for savings and other expenses?
    A. $196.00   B. $382.00   C. $649.40   D. $1960.00

28.___

29. Mr. Elsberg can pay back a loan of $1,800 from the city employees' retirement system if he pays back $36.69 every two weeks for two full years.
At the end of the two years, how much more than the original $1,800 he borrowed will Mr. Elsberg have paid back?
    A. $53.94   B. $107.88   C. $190.79   D. $214.76

29.___

30. Mrs. Nusbaum is a city employee, receiving a gross salary (salary before deductions) of $10,400. Every two weeks, the following deductions are taken out of her salary: Federal Income Tax, $81.32; FICA, $22.13; State Tax, $14.86; City Tax, $6.97; Health Insurance, $1.57.
If Mrs. Nusbaum's salary and deductions remained the same for a full calendar year, what would her NET salary (gross salary less deductions) be in that year?
    A. $3,298.10   B. $7,101.90
    C. $9,372.75   D. $10,273.15

30.___

KEY (CORRECT ANSWERS)

1. C	11. C	21. D
2. A	12. C	22. B
3. D	13. C	23. A
4. C	14. B	24. C
5. D	15. A	25. C
6. A	16. C	26. D
7. A	17. D	27. A
8. B	18. C	28. B
9. B	19. B	29. B
10. B	20. A	30. B

EXAMINATION SECTION

DIRECTIONS: Each question or incomplete statement is followed by several suggested answers or completions. Select the one that BEST answers the question or completes the statement. *PRINT THE LETTER OF THE CORRECT ANSWER IN THE SPACE AT THE RIGHT.*

Questions 1-5.

DIRECTIONS: Questions 1 through 5 are to be answered on the basis of the statement account shown below.

STATEMENT OF ACCOUNT

Regal Tools, Inc.
136 Culver Street
Cranston, R.I. 02910

TO: Vista, Inc.   DATE: March 31, 1986
     572 No. Copeland Ave.
     Pawtucket, R.I. 02800

DATE	ITEM	CHARGES	PAYMENTS AND CREDITS	BALANCE
	Previous Balance			785.35
March 8	Payment		785.35	----
12	Invoice 17-582	550 --		550.00
17	Invoice 17-692	700 --		1250.00
31	Payment		550.00	700.00

PAY LAST AMOUNT SHOWN IN BALANCE COLUMN

1. Which company is the customer?   1.___

2. What total amount was charged by the customer during March?   2.___

3. How much does the customer owe on March 31?   3.___

4. On which accounting schedule would Vista list Regal?   4.___

5. The terms on invoice 17-582 were 3/20, n/45.   5.___
    What was the CORRECT amount for which the check should
    have been written when payment was made?

6. Which item is NOT a source document?
   A(n)
   A. invoice   B. magnetic tape
   C. punched card   D. telephone conversation

   6.__

7. What is double-entry accounting?
   A. Journalizing and posting
   B. Recording debit and credit parts for a transaction
   C. Using carbon paper when preparing a source document
   D. Posting a debit or credit and computing the new
      account balance

   7.__

8. The balance in the asset account Supplies is $600. An
   ending inventory shows $200 of supplies on hand.
   The adjusting entry should be
   A. debit Supplies Expense for $200, credit Supplies
      for $200
   B. credit Supplies Expense for $200, debit Supplies
      for $200
   C. debit Supplies Expense for $400, credit Supplies
      for $400
   D. credit Supplies Expense for $400, debit Supplies
      for $400

   8.__

9. What is the purpose of preparing an Income Statement?
   To
   A. report the net income or net loss
   B. show the owner's claims against the assets
   C. prove that the accounting equation is in balance
   D. prove that the total debits equal the total credits

   9.__

10. Which account does NOT belong on the Income Statement?
    A. Salaries Payable
    B. Rental Revenue
    C. Advertising Expense
    D. Sales Returns and Allowances

    10.__

11. The source document for entries made in a Purchases
    Journal is a purchase
    A. order   B. requisition   C. invoice   D. register

    11.__

12. A business check guaranteed for payment by the bank is
    called a
    A. bank draft   B. certified check
    C. cashier's check   D. personal check

    12.__

13. The entry that closes the Purchases Account contains a
    A. debit to Purchases
    B. debit to Purchases Returns and Allowances
    C. credit to Purchases
    D. credit to Income and Expense Summary

    13.__

14. Which account would NOT appear on a Balance Sheet?
    A. Office Equipment   B. Transportation In
    C. Mortgage Payable   D. Supplies on Hand

    14.__

3

15. Which entry is made at the end of the fiscal period for the purpose of updating the Prepaid Insurance Account? _____ entry.
    A. Correcting   B. Closing   C. Adjusting   D. Reversing

15. ___

16. Which deduction from gross pay is NOT required by law?
    A. Hospitalization insurance
    B. FICA tax
    C. Federal income tax
    D. New York State income tax

16. ___

17. What is the last date on which a 2 percent cash discount can be taken for an invoice dated October 15 with terms of 2/10, n/30?
    A. October 15   B. October 17
    C. October 25   D. November 14

17. ___

18. Which item on the bank reconciliation statement would require the business to record a journal entry? A(n)
    A. deposit in transit   B. outstanding check
    C. canceled check   D. bank service charge

18. ___

19. Which is NOT an essential component of a computer? A(n)
    A. input device   B. central processor
    C. output device   D. telecommunicator

19. ___

20. Which group of accounts could appear on a post-closing trial balance?
    A. Petty Cash; Accounts Receivable; FICA Taxes Payable
    B. Office Furniture; Office Expense; Supplies on Hand
    C. Supplies Expense; Sales; Advertising Expense
    D. Sales Discount; Rent Expense; J. Smith, Drawing

20. ___

21. The withdrawals of cash by the owner are recorded in the owner's drawing account as a(n)
    A. adjusting entry   B. closing entry
    C. credit   D. debit

21. ___

22. An account in the General Ledger which shows a total of a related Subsidiary Ledger is referred to as a(n) _____ account.
    A. revenue   B. controlling
    C. temporary   D. owner's equity

22. ___

23.
    For Deposit Only
    Anthony Sill

23. ___

Which type of endorsement is shown above?
    A. Restrictive   B. Blank
    C. Full   D. Qualified

24. Which is a chronological record of all the transactions   24.__
    of a business?
       A. Worksheet   B. Income Statement
       C. Journal   D. Trial balance

25. Which error would NOT be revealed by the preparation of   25.__
    a trial balance?
       A. Posting of an entire transaction more than once
       B. Incorrectly pencil footing the balance of a general
          ledger account
       C. Posting a debit of $320 as $230
       D. Omitting an account with a balance

26. The Cash Receipts Journal is used to record the   26.__
       A. purchase of merchandise for cash
       B. purchase of merchandise on credit
       C. sale of merchandise for cash
       D. sale of merchandise on credit

27. On a systems flowchart, which symbol is commonly used   27.__
    to indicate the direction of the flow of work?
    A(n)
       A. arrow   B. circle   C. diamond   D. rectangle

28. Which account balance would be eliminated by a closing   28.__
    entry at the end of the fiscal period?
       A. Office Equipment   B. Owner's Drawing
       C. Owner's Capital   D. Mortgage Payable

29. In a data processing system, the handling and manipulation 29.__
    of data according to precise procedures is called
       A. input   B. processing
       C. storage   D. output

30. Which financial statement reflects the cumulative   30.__
    financial position of the business?
       A. Bank statement   B. Income statement
       C. Trial balance   D. Balance sheet

31. Which account should be credited when recording a cash   31.__
    proof showing an overage?
       A. Sales
       B. Cash
       C. Cash Short and Over
       D. Sales Returns and Allowances

32. In which section of the income statement would the   32.__
    purchases account be shown?
       A. Cost of Goods Sold   B. Income from Sales
       C. Operating Expenses   D. Other Expenses

33. What is an invoice?   33.__
    A(n)
       A. order for the shipment of goods
       B. order for the purchase of goods
       C. receipt for goods purchased
       D. statement listing goods purchased

34. A business uses a Sales Journal, a Purchases Journal, a Cash Receipts Journal, a Cash Payments Journal, and a General Journal.
In which journal would a credit memorandum received from a creditor be recorded?
____ Journal
A. Sales   B. Purchases
C. General   D. Cash Receipts

34.___

35. Which account is debited to record a weekly payroll?
A. Employees Income Tax Payable
B. FICA Taxes Payable
C. General Expense
D. Salaries Expense

35.___

KEY (CORRECT ANSWERS)

1. Vista, Inc.
2. $1,250
3. $700
4. Accts. Payable
5. $533.50

6. D
7. B
8. C
9. A
10. A

11. C
12. B
13. C
14. D
15. C

16. A
17. C
18. D
19. D
20. A

21. D
22. B
23. A
24. C
25. A

26. C
27. A
28. B
29. B
30. D

31. C
32. A
33. D
34. C
35. D

EXAMINATION SECTION

TEST 1

DIRECTIONS: Each question or incomplete statement is followed by
several suggested answers or completions. Select the
one that BEST answers the question or completes the
statement. *PRINT THE LETTER OF THE CORRECT ANSWER IN
THE SPACE AT THE RIGHT.*

Questions 1-5.

DIRECTIONS: Questions 1 through 5 are to be answered on the basis
of the following information.

     The balance on our bank statement is $6,842.50. The bank had
made a service charge of $4.50. Our check stubs reveal a final
balance of $5,747.50. A comparison of the check stubs with the bank
statement indicated that a deposit we had mailed on the 29th for $585
had not been recorded by the monthly closing. Four checks which we
had made out ($1,001, $645, $38.50, and a certified check for $1,200)
had not been cleared by the monthly closing.

1. The effect of the deposit in transit is to _____ balance.　　1.___
    A. *increase* the final check stub
    B. *decrease* the final check stub
    C. *increase* the bank
    D. *decrease* the bank

2. The effect of the bank service charge is to _____ balance.　　2.___
    A. *increase* the final check stub
    B. *decrease* the final check stub
    C. *increase* the bank
    D. *decrease* the bank

3. The CORRECTED check stub balance after reconciliation is　　3.___
    A. $5,743   B. $5,752   C. $6,337   D. $6,843

4. The TOTAL of the outstanding checks to be subtracted from　　4.___
the bank balance is
    A. $484.50   B. $1,684.50 C. $2,269.50 D. $2,885.50

5. The CORRECTED bank balance after reconciliation is　　5.___
    A. $5,743   B. $5,789   C. $6,843   D. $7,428

Questions 6-8.

DIRECTIONS: Questions 6 through 8 are to be answered on the basis of the worksheet below, which is for the first quarter of the Argo Taxi Company.

ARGO TAXI CO., INC
WORKSHEET
FOR QUARTER ENDED 3/31/

	TRIAL BALANCE		ADJUSTMENTS		INCOME STATEMENT		BALANCE SHEET	
Cash	17000						17000	
Oil Products Inventory	5000			3600			1400	
Prepaid Insurance	1000			680			320	
Automobiles	105000						105000	
Allow. for Depreciation of Autos		28000		3750				31750
Maintenance Equipment	20000						20000	
Allow. for Dep. of Maintenance Equip.		7000		500				7500
Accounts Payable		1200						1200
Dividends Payable		2000						2000
Capital Stock		55000						55000
Retained Earnings		13200						13200
Fares Income		80000				80000		
Miscellaneous Expenses	4500				4500			
Rent Expense	1500				1500			
Repair Expense	5200				5200			
Salary Expense	24000				24000			
	192200	192200						
Oil Products Expense			3600		3600			
Insurance Expense			680		680			
Depreciation of Automobiles Exp.			3750		3750			
Dep. of Maintenance Equip.			500		500			
			8530	8530	48730	80000	152720	121450
Federal Income Taxes					7817.50			7817.50
Net Profit after Income Taxes					23452.50			23452.50
					80000	80000	152720	152720

6. The balance of the Automobiles account after the June adjustment is
A. $8,750   B. $23,000   C. $31,750   D. $105,000

6.___

7. The book value of the asset Maintenance Equipment, after adjusting entries, is
A. $7,500   B. $12,500   C. $13,000   D. $20,000

7.___

8. Assuming that the entire net profit after taxes was transferred to Retained Earnings, the balance of the Retained Earnings account would be
A. $10,252.50   B. $13,200
C. $23,452.50   D. $36,652.50

8.___

9. The TOTAL operating expenses for the quarter were
A. $13,530   B. $48,730   C. $121,450   D. $192,200

9.___

10. Closing entries are prepared from _____ columns.
A. Trial Balance   B. Adjustment
C. Income Statement   D. Balance Sheet

10.___

11. When sales taxes are collected from cash customers, the account credited is
A. Sales Taxes Payable   B. Sales Taxes
C. Cash   D. Accounts Payable

11.___

3 (#1)

12. What type of data processing equipment would arrange   12.___
    punched cards alphabetically?
        A. Card punch   B. Card verifier
        C. Sorter   D. Tabulator

13. _____ tax is affected by the number of exemptions claimed   13.___
    by the employee.
        A. State Unemployment Insurance
        B. Federal Unemployment Insurance
        C. FICA
        D. Federal income

14. The merchandise turnover is found by dividing _____   14.___
    merchandise inventory.
        A. net sales by ending
        B. net sales by average
        C. cost of goods sold by average
        D. cost of goods sold by ending

15. The process of summarizing the income and expense accounts 15.___
    and transferring the net result to the Retained Earnings
    account is known as
        A. adjusting the accounts
        B. reversing the accounts
        C. closing the ledger
        D. preparing a post-closing trial balance

16. An example of a fixed asset is   16.___
        A. equipment   B. merchandise inventory
        C. cash   D. prepaid insurance

17. Determining that the amount of cash on hand agrees with   17.___
    the balance of the cash account is known as
        A. recording
        B. proving cash
        C. reconciling the bank statement
        D. establishing the petty cash fund

18. The balance in the Accounts Receivable controlling account 18.___
    on December 31 is $20,500. The balance in the Allowance
    for Bad Debts account is $750 after adjustments.
    The amount believed to be collectible from customers is
        A. $750   B. $19,750   C. $20,500   D. $21,250

19. The FIRST record of any transaction of a business is made   19.___
    in the
        A. ledger   B. account
        C. journal   D. balance sheet

20. A decrease in owner's capital that results from a   20.___
    business transaction is called
        A. income   B. expense   C. asset   D. liability

21. The difference between the sales and the cost of goods sold is called
    A. net sales
    B. sales returns
    C. gross profit on sales
    D. sales discount
                                                 21.___

22. A customer sent a check for $50 in partial payment of her account.
What would be the effect of erroneously posting the check as a debit to the customer's account?
    A. *Overstatement* of the total of the Schedule of Accounts Receivable
    B. *Understatement* of the Accounts Receivable controlling account
    C. *Overstatement* of the Accounts Receivable controlling account
    D. *Understatement* of the total of the Schedule of Accounts Receivable
         22.___

23. In the absence of any statement in the partnership agreement as to the manner of sharing profits and losses, such profits and losses will be shared
    A. equally
    B. according to investments
    C. according to work performed
    D. according to sales
         23.___

24. At the end of the year, which account should be closed into the Income and Expense Summary account?
    A. Petty Cash
    B. Depreciation of Furniture and Fixtures
    C. Allowance for Bad Debts
    D. Notes Payable
         24.___

25. On an Income Statement, losses from bad debts will appear as a(n)
    A. operating expense
    B. deduction from Accounts Receivable
    C. addition to the cost of goods sold
    D. deduction from the cost of goods sold
         25.___

KEY (CORRECT ANSWERS)

1. C	6. D	11. A	16. A	21. C
2. B	7. B	12. C	17. B	22. A
3. A	8. D	13. D	18. B	23. A
4. B	9. B	14. C	19. C	24. B
5. A	10. C	15. C	20. B	25. A

TEST 2

DIRECTIONS: Each question or incomplete statement is followed by several suggested answers or completions. Select the one that BEST answers the question or completes the statement. *PRINT THE LETTER OF THE CORRECT ANSWER IN THE SPACE AT THE RIGHT.*

1. A bookkeeping worksheet is prepared   1.___
   A. to be used as a source document
   B. to distribute to the stockholders at the end of the year
   C. as an aid in the preparation of financial statements
   D. to be used as a financial statement

2. When a set of books for a partnership is opened, the CORRECT procedure is to set up   2.___
   A. a capital account for each partner
   B. a capital account for each partner except *silent* partners
   C. one capital account that would show the combined investment of the partners
   D. an account showing stock already subscribed

3. At the end of the fiscal period, it is determined that the interest owed and not paid on the mortgage amounts to $420. This amount will be debited to   3.___
   A. Interest Expense   B. Mortgage Payable
   C. Interest Receivable   D. Interest Income

4. Income that has been earned but not yet received is referred to as _____ income.   4.___
   A. deferred   B. accrued   C. unearned   D. prepaid

5. The account Mortgage Payable is a(n)   5.___
   A. current liability   B. prepaid expense
   C. accrued expense   D. fixed liability

6. Under the cash basis of keeping books, all items of income are recorded when   6.___
   A. paid   B. billed   C. received   D. ordered

7. A financial statement prepared by a data processing system is an example of   7.___
   A. a source document   B. output
   C. a flowchart   D. input

8. On an income statement, net sales minus cost of goods sold is the   8.___
   A. gross profit
   B. merchandise available for sale
   C. net operating profit
   D. net profit before taxes

9. Allowance for Depreciation of Delivery Equipment is a(n)   9.___
   _____ account.
       A. liability   B. expense   C. accrual   D. valuation

10. When the totals of the two columns of a Trial Balance are   10.___
    equal, it proves that
        A. all debits and credits have been posted to the proper
           accounts
        B. there have been no offsetting errors
        C. no entries have been omitted
        D. equal amounts of debits and credits have been posted

11. The TOTAL of the Sales Journal is posted as a debit to   11.___
        A. Accounts Receivable   B. Accounts Payable
        C. Sales   D. Cash

12. Unexpired insurance is recorded as a debit to   12.___
        A. Insurance Receivable   B. Prepaid Insurance
        C. Insurance Payable   D. Insurance Expense

13. The cost price of a fixed asset minus the Allowance for   13.___
    Depreciation is known as its _____ value.
        A. cash   B. par   C. market   D. book

14. The payment in cash by The Lake Corporation on April 1,   14.___
    1988 of a dividend declared and recorded on March 10,
    1988 results in
        A. a decrease in assets and a decrease in capital
        B. both an increase and a decrease in assets
        C. a decrease in assets and a decrease in liabilities
        D. a decrease in liabilities and an increase in capital

15. Current assets minus current liabilities equals   15.___
        A. current ratio   B. current turnover
        C. merchandise turnover   D. working capital

16. The proprietor withdrew cash for his personal use.   16.___
    The effect on the fundamental bookkeeping equation is to
        A. *increase* assets and decrease owner's worth
        B. *increase* assets and increase owner's worth
        C. *decrease* assets and decrease liabilities
        D. *decrease* assets and decrease owner's worth

17. A payment for gasoline and oil was incorrectly debited to 17.___
    the Delivery Equipment account instead of to the Delivery
    Expense account.
    This error, if not corrected, would result in
        A. understatement of the total assets
        B. no effect on the net profit
        C. an understatement of the net profit
        D. an overstatement of the net profit

18. A bookkeeper made an entry debiting the Bad Debts Expense   18.___
    account and crediting the Allowance for Bad Debts account.
    The credit represents a(n)
    A. *increase* in the liabilities
    B. *increase* in the net worth
    C. *decrease* in the value of the assets
    D. *decrease* in the liabilities

19. Adjusting entries are NORMALLY made   19.___
    A. before the Trial Balance is taken
    B. whenever price changes occur in inventory costs
    C. at the beginning of each fiscal period
    D. at the end of the current fiscal period

20. The declaration of a cash dividend by the Yule Corporation   20.___
    will result in a(n)
    A. *increase* in assets and an increase in liabilities
    B. *increase* in liabilities and a decrease in capital
    C. *decrease* in assets and a decrease in liabilities
    D. *decrease* in assets and a decrease in capital

21.   21.___

Accounts Payable

19						19					
May	31		CP6	178	00	May	31			P3	320	00
	31		J4	80	00						
June	2		J5	75	00						

    The above account was taken from the General Ledger of
    Clarke & Scott.
    The above account is classified as a
    A. fixed liability   B. contingent asset
    C. deferred asset   D. current liability

22. When a corporation declares a dividend on its stock,   22.___
    the account debited is
    A. Dividends Payable   B. Retained Earnings
    C. Capital Stock   D. Stock Subscriptions

23. The payroll tax for the State unemployment insurance   23.___
    is paid by
    A. the employee *only*
    B. both the employee and the employer
    C. the employer *only*
    D. the insurance company

24. Which of the following can NOT be used as input into   24.___
    a computer?
    A. Punched card   B. Magnetic tape
    C. Punched paper tape   D. Printer

25. A diagram of a bookkeeping operation through a computerized 25. ___
    system is called a
    A. floor plan   B. worksheet
    C. flowchart   D. CPU

———

KEY (CORRECT ANSWERS)

1. C		11. A
2. A		12. B
3. A		13. D
4. B		14. C
5. D		15. D
6. C		16. D
7. B		17. D
8. A		18. C
9. D		19. D
10. D		20. B

21. D
22. B
23. C
24. D
25. C

———

TEST 3

DIRECTIONS: Each question or incomplete statement is followed by several suggested answers or completions. Select the one that BEST answers the question or completes the statement. *PRINT THE LETTER OF THE CORRECT ANSWER IN THE SPACE AT THE RIGHT.*

1. The process of transferring information from the journal to the ledger is called
   A. journalizing   B. posting
   C. closing   D. balancing

   1.___

2. Which is NOT an asset account?
   A. Supplies on Hand   B. Prepaid Insurance
   C. Office Equipment   D. Sales

   2.___

3. Which journal entries are used at the end of each accounting period to clear the balances from the temporary accounts so that these accounts may be used in accumulating data for preparing the next period's statement.
   ____ entries.
   A. Correcting   B. Closing
   C. Adjusting   D. Opening

   3.___

4. The verification of the equality of debits and credits in the General Ledger is called a
   A. trial balance   B. schedule
   C. statement   D. worksheet

   4.___

5. Which account would NOT be listed on the Balance Sheet as a current liability?
   A. Accounts Payable
   B. Sales Taxes Payable
   C. Mortgage Payable
   D. FICA Taxes Payable

   5.___

6. Debts owed by a business enterprise are referred to as
   A. capital   B. income   C. assets   D. liabilities

   6.___

7. If insurance premiums were recorded as an asset when paid, the adjusting entry needed to record the expired insurance would require a debit to which account?
   A. Miscellaneous Expense   B. Prepaid Insurance
   C. Insurance Expense   D. John Green, Capital

   7.___

8. A diagram showing the sequence of steps involved in an automated data processing procedure is called a
   A. flowchart   B. source document
   C. coding sheet   D. spreadsheet

   8.___

9. If a business enterprise paid $3,000 to its creditors on   9.___
   account, what was the effect of the transaction on the
   accounting equation?
   A(n)
      A. *increase* in an asset, an increase in a liability
      B. *decrease* in an asset, a decrease in a liability
      C. *increase* in an asset, an increase in capital
      D. *increase* in one asset, a decrease in another asset

10. Which three steps of an automated data processing system   10.___
    are listed in the PROPER order?
      A. Input, storage, process
      B. Process, data origination, output
      C. Output, input, storage
      D. Input, process, output

11. The Merchandise Inventory account is GENERALLY adjusted   11.___
      A. when inventory is purchased
      B. when inventory is sold
      C. at the end of the accounting period
      D. at the beginning of each month

12. Which transaction is recorded in the Sales Journal?   12.___
    The sale of
      A. merchandise for cash
      B. merchandise on account
      C. vacant land (plant asset) for cash
      D. vacant land (plant asset) on account

13. Which is an example of a transposition error?   13.___
    Recording $450 as
      A. $540   B. $4,500.00   C. $455   D. $4.50

14. The accounting equation is CORRECTLY stated as   14.___
      A. Owner's Equity = Assets + Liabilities
      B. Owner's Equity - Assets = Liabilities
      C. Owner's Equity = Liabilities - Assets
      D. Assets = Liabilities + Owner's Equity

15. The Wage and Tax statement, Form W-2, is a form which   15.___
    shows
      A. a listing of deductions taken from an employee's
         salary
      B. an end-of-year listing of total wages and income tax
         and FICA withholdings
      C. the bonds purchased for an employee by an employer
      D. the marital status of an employee and the number of
         allowances claimed

16. A set of instructions which guides the processing of   16.___
    data by an electronic computer is called a
      A. file   B. diagram   C. program   D. record

17. An invoice is dated June 3. Terms of the sale are n/45.   17.___
    What is the LAST date for payment?
      A. June 30   B. July 17   C. July 18   D. July 19

18. The accounting equation is summarized in the   18.___
    A. Balance Sheet
    B. Trial Balance
    C. Income Statement
    D. Schedule of Accounts Payable

19. The Accounts Payable Subsidiary Ledger contains the   19.___
    amounts
    A. owed to the business by charge customers
    B. owed by the business to creditors
    C. of all cash purchases of merchandise
    D. of all sales discounts

20. Which procedure is followed in a journalless accounting   20.___
    system for handling accounts receivable?
    A. A trial balance must be prepared daily.
    B. Debits do not equal credits at the end of the
       accounting period when all postings have been made.
    C. Individual sales are recorded in a multicolumn Sales
       Journal instead of in a one-column Sales Journal.
    D. Posting to customers' accounts is made directly from
       the sales invoices.

21. _____ is a voluntary payroll deduction.   21.___
    A. FICA tax   B. Credit union savings
    C. Federal withholding tax   D. State income tax

22. On a worksheet, if the Trial Balance debit column is   22.___
    larger than the Trial Balance credit column, it indicates
    a(n)
    A. net income   B. net loss
    C. error   D. decrease in capital

23. In the General Ledger, the controlling account that   23.___
    summarizes the activities in the Customer's Ledger is
    called
    A. Accounts Receivable   B. Accounts Payable
    C. Purchases   D. Sales

24. The balance of the Insurance Expense account in the   24.___
    Income Statement debit column on the worksheet represents
    the
    A. insurance expired during the fiscal period
    B. face value of all insurance policies
    C. value of the prepaid insurance at the end of the
       fiscal period
    D. cash value of all insurance policies

25. A fee paid to the bank when securing a cashier's check   25.___
    should be recorded by a debit to _____ and a credit to
    _____.
    A. Petty Cash; Cash
    B. Miscellaneous Expense; Bank Charges
    C. Accounts Receivable; Cash
    D. Miscellaneous Expense; Cash

KEY (CORRECT ANSWERS)

1. B	11. C
2. D	12. B
3. B	13. A
4. A	14. D
5. C	15. B
6. D	16. C
7. C	17. C
8. A	18. A
9. B	19. B
10. D	20. D

21. B
22. C
23. A
24. A
25. D

_____

TEST 4

DIRECTIONS: Each question or incomplete statement is followed by several suggested answers or completions. Select the one that BEST answers the question or completes the statement. *PRINT THE LETTER OF THE CORRECT ANSWER IN THE SPACE AT THE RIGHT.*

1. A 60-day promissory note dated April 12 will be due on June
   A. 11   B. 12   C. 13   D. 14

   1.____

2. Failure to set up an allowance for doubtful accounts at the end of 1988 will result in an _____ 1988.
   A. *understatement* of net profit for
   B. *overstatement* of net profit for
   C. *understatement* of assets at the end of
   D. *overstatement* of liabilities at the end of

   2.____

3. Which error will cause the trial balance to be out of balance?
   A. Forgetting to post from the Sales Journal to the H. Allen account in the Accounts Receivable Ledger
   B. Failing to record the purchase of a desk
   C. Incorrectly totaling the Purchase Journal
   D. Posting the $1,250 total of the accounts receivable column in the Cash Receipts Journal as $1,520

   3.____

4. The checkbook balance on May 2, at the start of the day, was $1,500. During the day, a deposit of $75 was made, and checks for $100 and $50 were written.
   What was the checkbook balance at the end of the day?
   A. $1,275   B. $1,425   C. $1,575   D. $1,725

   4.____

5. Data about Accounts Receivable to be fed into an automatic data processing system is often recorded in the form of
   A. statements of account
   B. punched cards
   C. schedule of accounts receivable
   D. sales journals

   5.____

6. A purchase of merchandise on credit results in a(n) _____ in assets and a(n) _____ in liabilities.
   A. increase; increase   B. increase; decrease
   C. decrease; decrease   D. decrease; increase

   6.____

7. During her vacation, Harriet Miller, age 45, was injured while driving her own car.
   For part of the 5 weeks she was unable to work, cash benefits MOST likely would be paid to her under
   A. Workmen's Compensation
   B. the Social Security Administration
   C. State Disability Benefits Insurance
   D. Unemployment Insurance

   7.____

8. The book value of a share of stock of a corporation may   8.___
   be found by
   A. dividing the net worth of the corporation by the
      number of shares of stock
   B. dividing the total amount of stock of the corporation
      by the number of shares of stock
   C. looking at the amount shown on the stock certificate
   D. looking at the price of the stock on the stock
      exchange page of the daily newspaper

9. In a business, which are MOST likely to be prepared by   9.___
   automatic data processing?
   A. Sales invoices
   B. Inspection reports by the night watchman
   C. Business correspondence (letters)
   D. Applications for employment

10. The entry recording the estimated depreciation for the   10.___
    year results in a(n) _____ in capital.
    A. increase in liabilities and a decrease
    B. decrease in liabilities and an increase
    C. increase in assets and an increase
    D. decrease in assets and a decrease

11. The balance of the Accounts Receivable controlling   11.___
    account would be different from the total of the Accounts
    Receivable Schedule if the bookkeeper
    A. made an error in totaling the Sales Journal and
       posted the incorrect total
    B. failed to record a sale made to S. Charles
    C. recorded the receipt of a check from a customer but
       neglected to record the cash discount
    D. added an invoice incorrectly and entered the incorrect
       total in the Sales Journal

12. Credits in the Notes Payable account USUALLY originate   12.___
    in the _____ Journal.
    A. Purchase   B. Cash Receipts
    C. Cash Payments   D. General

13. On the books of the seller, the deduction granted to a   13.___
    customer for early payment of the invoice is called a
    _____ discount.
    A. retail   B. purchase   C. trade   D. sales

14. A firm started the year with $25 worth of office supplies. 14.___
    During the year, the firm purchased $65 worth of office
    supplies. A count of the office supplies at the end of
    the year showed that $20 worth was still on hand.
    What was the TOTAL cost of the office supplies which the
    firm must have used during the year?
    A. $45   B. $60   C. $70   D. $110

15. A payroll check prepared by a computer is an example of _____ data processing _____.
    A. electronic; input B. electronic; output
    C. manual; output   D. manual; input

15.___

16. A sale of $250 was made subject to a 7% sales tax. To record the sale CORRECTLY, the credits should be Sales Income
    A. $250, Sales Taxes $17.50
    B. $250, Sales Taxes Payable $17.50
    C. $267.50, Sales Taxes $17.50
    D. $267.50, Sales Taxes Payable $17.50

16.___

17. In order to determine which checks are outstanding, the bookkeeper should compare the
    A. cancelled checks with the stubs in the checkbook
    B. cancelled checks with the checks listed in the bank statement
    C. check stubs with entries made in the Cash Payments Journal
    D. checkbook deposits with entries made in the Cash Receipts Journal

17.___

18. In a sale on credit to B. Benson, the bookkeeper, by mistake, posted to the B. Boyers account. The error will PROBABLY be discovered when
    A. the schedule of the subsidiary ledger does not agree with the controlling account
    B. the trial balance does not balance
    C. B. Boyers receives his monthly statement
    D. the bookkeeper receives monthly statements from creditors

18.___

19. Which does a person receive as evidence of part ownership in a corporation?
    A
    A. certificate of incorporation
    B. stock certificate
    C. bond
    D. charter

19.___

20. The count of merchandise inventory on hand at the end of the year was overstated. This error will result in an _____ the year.
    A. *overstatement* of profit for
    B. *understatement* of profit for
    C. *overstatement* of liabilities at the end of
    D. *understatement* of assets at the end of

20.___

21. The Accounts Receivable account is an example of a _____ account.
    A. subsidiary   B. controlling
    C. fixed asset   D. valuation

21.___

22. The _____ check provides space for stating the purpose for which the check is written.
     A. cashier's B. certified C. preferred D. voucher   22.___

23. If the assets of a firm at the end of the year were greater than the assets at the beginning of the year, then which statement would be CORRECT?   23.___
     A. The firm made a profit for the year.
     B. The firm was well managed for the year.
     C. The capital of the firm was greater at the end of the year.
     D. More information is needed before arriving at a conclusion.

24. Which is a legal characteristic of a general partnership? _____ liability.   24.___
     A. Long-term   B. Unlimited
     C. Contingent   D. Deferred

25. The term *double entry bookkeeping* means that, for each transaction, an entry is made   25.___
     A. in the journal and also in the ledger
     B. in the general ledger and also in a subsidiary ledger
     C. on the debit side of one account and on the credit side of another account
     D. on a business paper and also in the books

KEY (CORRECT ANSWERS)

1. A		11. A	
2. B		12. D	
3. D		13. D	
4. B		14. C	
5. B		15. B	
6. A		16. B	
7. C		17. A	
8. A		18. C	
9. A		19. B	
10. D		20. A	

21. B
22. D
23. D
24. B
25. C

EXAMINATION SECTION
TEST 1

DIRECTIONS: Each question or incomplete statement is followed by several suggested answers or completions. Select the one that BEST answers the question or completes the statement. *PRINT THE LETTER OF THE CORRECT ANSWER IN THE SPACE AT THE RIGHT.*

Questions 1-7.

DIRECTIONS: Questions 1 through 7 are to be answered on the basis of the following income statement.

Laura Lee's Bridal Shop
Income Statement
For the Year Ended December 31, 1995

Revenue:		
New & Used Bridal Gowns & Accessories		$55,000
Expenses:		
Advertisement Expense	$ 2,000	
Salaries Expense	12,000	
Dry cleaning & Alterations	10,000	
Utilities	1,500	
Total Expenses		25,500
Net Income		$29,500

1. What is the period of time covered by this income statement?
   A. January-December 1994
   B. December 1995
   C. January 1994-December 1995
   D. January-December 1995

   1.____

2. What is the source of the revenue?
   A. New and used bridal gowns, advertisements, salaries, dry cleaning, and utilities
   B. Advertisements, salaries, dry cleaning, alterations, and utilities
   C. New and used bridal gowns and accessories
   D. Net income

   2.____

3. What is the total revenue?
   A. $25,500   B. $55,000   C. $29,500   D. $79,500

   3.____

4. Which of the following are expenses?
   A. Salaries
   B. New and used bridal gowns and accessories
   C. Revenue
   D. New and used bridal gowns, advertisements, and dry cleaning

   4.____

5. What are the total expenses?   5.___
   A. $55,000   B. $29,500   C. $79,500   D. $25,500

6. There is a resulting net income because   6.___
   A. total revenue and total expenses are combined
   B. net income is greater than total revenue
   C. the total revenue is greater than total expenses
   D. the total revenue is less than total expenses

7. Is this statement an interim statement?   7.___
   A. *Yes*, because it covers an entire accounting period
   B. *No*, because it covers an entire accounting period
   C. *Yes*, because it covers a period of less than a year
   D. *No*, because it covers a period of more than a year

8. What is the name of the accounting report that may show   8.___
   either a net profit or a net loss for an accounting
   period?
   A. Income statement   B. Balance sheet
   C. Statement of capital   D. Classified balance sheet

9. What are the two main parts of the body of the income   9.___
   statement?
   A. Cash and Capital   B. Revenue and Expenses
   C. Liabilities and Capital   D. Assets and Notes Payable

10. If total revenue exceeds total expenses for an accounting   10.___
    period, what is the difference called?
    A. Gross income   B. Total liabilities
    C. Total assets   D. Net income

11. In the body of a balance sheet, what are the three   11.___
    sections called?
    A. Assets and liabilities
    B. Cash, liabilities, and revenue
    C. Assets, liabilities, and capital
    D. Revenue, assets, and capital

12. What business record shows the results of the proprietor's   12.___
    borrowing assets from the business, usually in anticipa-
    tion of profits?
    A. Proprietor's withdrawals
    B. Accounts payable
    C. Liabilities and Capital
    D. Total liabilities

Questions 13-24.

DIRECTIONS: For each transaction given for Mona's Magic Moments
              Hair Salon in Questions 13 through 24, identify
              which journal the transaction should be recorded, in.

13. April 1: Mona, the owner, paid the month's rent - $600.00; 13.___
    check no. 356.
    A. General   B. Cash disbursements
    C. Purchases   D. Sales

14. April 6: the salon purchased $300.00 worth of styling   14.___
    products on account from Pomme de Terre Company.
    A. Cash disbursements   B. General
    C. Sales   D. Purchases

15. April 8: sold $100.00 worth of hair products on account   15.___
    to Mrs. Angela Bray.
    A. Sales   B. Purchases
    C. Cash disbursements D. General

16. April 11: the owner, Mona Ramen, withdrew $80.00 of   16.___
    styling products for personal use.
    A. Sales   B. Cash receipts
    C. General   D. Cash disbursements

17. April 13: paid Pomme de Terre Company $300.00 on   17.___
    account; check 357.
    A. Purchases   B. Cash disbursements
    C. Cash receipts   D. General

18. April 15: cash sales to date were $4,607.00.   18.___
    A. Cash disbursements B. Purchases
    C. Sales   D. General

19. April 17: issued credit slip #17 to Mrs. Angela Bray   19.___
    for $25.00 for merchandise returned.
    A. Cash disbursements B. Cash receipts
    C. Sales   D. General

20. April 19: paid electric bill for $250.00; check no. 358. 20.___
    A. Cash disbursements B. Purchases
    C. General   D. Cash receipts

21. April 21: received $75.00 from Mrs. Angela Bray for   21.___
    balance due on account.
    A. Sales   B. Cash disbursements
    C. Cash receipts   D. Purchases

22. April 23: sold $88.00 of hair products on account to   22.___
    Ms. Tania Alioto.
    A. Purchases   B. Sales
    C. Cash disbursements D. Cash receipts

23. April 27: purchased $500.00 of equipment from Salon   23.___
    Stylings Merchandisers on account.
    A. Cash disbursements B. Sales
    C. General   D. Purchases

24. April 30: cash sales to date were $5023.00.   24.__
    A. Purchases   B. Sales
    C. Cash receipts   D. General

Questions 25-30.

DIRECTIONS: Questions 25 through 30 are to be answered on the basis of the following ledger for a barbecue take-out restaurant owned and operated by Ruby Joiner.

Cash		Accounts Receivable		Delivery Equipment	
450	150	360	170	5,000	
212	125	250	100	4,000	
328	440	165	120	3,000	
172	125	100	60		
250	70				
275	150				
325	50				

Supplies		Ruby Joiner, Capital		Accounts Payable	
40			8,200	10	600
65			2,000	15	300
30			2,097		200
25					

Ruby Joiner, Drawing		Advertising Expense		Delivery Income	
225		40			400
175		45			350
200					250
					100

Trucking Expense		Telephone Expense	
100		80	
50		40	
		20	

25. What is the balance on the Cash account shown above?   25.__
    A. 2,012.00 B. 1,110.00 C. 3,122.00 D. 902.00

26. What is the balance on the Accounts receivable account   26.__
shown above?
    A. 425.00   B. 875.00   C. 450.00   D. 1315.00

27. What is the balance on the Accounts payable account   27.__
shown above?
    A. 1100.00   B. 1075.00   C. 25.00   D. 1125.00

28. Which of the above accounts has a balance of 1100.00?   28.__
    A. Accounts payable   B. Delivery income
    C. Cash   D. Delivery equipment

29. Which of the above accounts has a balance of 12,000.00?   29.___
    A. Ruby Joiner, Capital
    B. Cash and Accounts receivable combined
    C. Delivery equipment
    D. None of the accounts

30. If you made a balance sheet out of the information listed   30.___
    above, Ruby Joiner's total assets would be
    A. 14,472.00 B. 12,297.00 C. 13,392.00 D. 13,487.00

Questions 31-34.

DIRECTIONS: Questions 31 through 34 are to be answered on the
             basis of the following information, to be included
             on a checking deposit ticket.

Five $20 bills; 11 $10 bills; 6 $5 bills; 47 $1 bills; 200 half
dollars; 120 quarters; 112 dimes; 320 nickels; 67 pennies.
Second National Bank (73-124) check of 152.34; Bank of the Midwest
(13-298) check of 68.37; Great National Bank (32-165) check of
185.06.

31. What is the TOTAL currency for this deposit?   31.___
    A. $387   B. $287   C. $444.87   D. $157.87

32. What is the TOTAL coin for this deposit?   32.___
    A. $387   B. $287   C. $444.87   D. $157.87

33. What is the check total for this deposit?   33.___
    A. $692.77   B. $406   C. $405.77   D. $850.64

34. What is the TOTAL deposit?   34.___
    A. $444.87   B. $692.77   C. $851   D. $850.64

Questions 35-37.

DIRECTIONS: Questions 35 through 37 are to be answered on the
             basis of the following petty cash journal.

Date	Receipt No.	To Whom Paid	For What	Acct.#	Amount
10/2	1	Anna Jones - Mail	Postage	548	13.50
10/2	2	Jim Collins	Telegram	525	5.75
10/4	3	Anna Jones - Mail	Postage	548	13.50
10/5	4	Lucky Stores	Coffee	515	7.34
10/6	5	Tom Allen	Lunch w/customer	525	11.38

35. What is the TOTAL disbursement from this fund for the   35.___
    time period 10/1 through 10/6?
    A. $51.47   B. $40.09   C. $61.47   D. $26.59

36. How much money was disbursed to Account #548 during the   36.__
    time period 10/1-10/16?
        A. $51.47   B. $26   C. $27   D. $34.34

37. If the fund began the month with a total of $100.00, what   37.__
    amount was left in the fund at the end of business on
    10/5?
        A. $48.53   B. $59.91   C. $51.47   D. $40.09

Questions 38-40.

DIRECTIONS: Questions 38 through 40 are to be answered on the
               basis of the following information.

    A promissory note dated December 1, 1995, bearing interest at
a rate of 12% and due in 90 days, is sent to a creditor. The face
value of the note is $900.

38. What is the due date of the promissory note?   38.__
        A. January 15, 1996   B. March 1, 1996
        C. February 1, 1996   D. December 31, 1995

39. What is the TOTAL interest that will be earned on the note?   39.__
        A. $27   B. $270   C. $108   D. $10.80

40. What interest will be earned on the note for the old   40.__
    accounting period (December 1-31)?
        A. $90   B. $36   C. $9   D. $3.60

_____

KEY (CORRECT ANSWERS)

1. D	11. C	21. C	31. B
2. C	12. A	22. B	32. D
3. B	13. B	23. D	33. C
4. A	14. D	24. B	34. D
5. D	15. A	25. D	35. A
6. C	16. C	26. A	36. C
7. B	17. B	27. B	37. B
8. A	18. C	28. B	38. B
9. B	19. D	29. C	39. A
10. D	20. A	30. D	40. C

_____

TEST 2

DIRECTIONS: Each question or incomplete statement is followed by
several suggested answers or completions. Select the
one that BEST answers the question or completes the
statement. *PRINT THE LETTER OF THE CORRECT ANSWER IN
THE SPACE AT THE RIGHT.*

Questions 1-4.

DIRECTIONS: Questions 1 through 4 are to be answered on the basis
of the following information, to be included in a
deposit slip.

    14 twenty dollar bills   63 quarters
    52 ten dollar bills   22 dimes
    12 five dollar bills   44 nickels
    43 one dollar bills   70 pennies

    Checks: $236.34 and $129.72

1. What is the TOTAL amount of currency for this deposit?   1.___
    A. $923.85   B. $1269.06   C. $903.00   D. $1299.91

2. What is the TOTAL amount of coin for this deposit?   2.___
    A. $20.85   B. $923.85   C. $903.00   D. $1299.91

3. What is the TOTAL amount of check for this deposit?   3.___
    A. $20.85   B. $366.06   C. $1299.91   D. $903.00

4. What is the TOTAL deposit for this slip?   4.___
    A. $1269.06   B. $903.00   C. $923.85   D. $1299.91

Questions 5-7.

DIRECTIONS: Questions 5 through 7 are to be answered on the basis
of the following information.

    Angela Martinez' last check stub balance was $675.50. Her bank
statement balance dated April 30 was $652.00. A $250 deposit was in
transit on that date. Outstanding checks were as follows: No. 127,
$65.00; No. 129, $203.50; No. 130, $50.00. The bank service charge
for the month was $5.00.

5. What was Angela Martinez' available checkbook balance on   5.___
    April 30?
    A. $652.00   B. $338.50   C. $588.50   D. $675.50

6. In order to reconcile her checkbook balance with her bank
   statement balance, what must Angela Martinez do?
   A. Add her checkbook balance to the balance on her bank
      statement
   B. Subtract her checkbook balance from the balance on
      her bank statement
   C. Ignore her checkbook balance and adopt the balance
      on her bank statement
   D. Adjust the checkbook balance by adding deposits and
      debiting outstanding checks and charges

6.___

7. The check stub balance referred to in the problem refers
   to the
   A. last check Angela Martinez recorded in her checkbook
   B. amount of money left in Angela Martinez' account
      according to her own calculations based on the checks,
      charges, and deposits she has written and recorded
   C. amount of money left in Angela Martinez' account
      according to the bank's calculations based on the
      checks, charges, and deposits posted to her account
   D. number of checks left in her checkbook

7.___

Questions 8-9.

DIRECTIONS: Questions 8 and 9 are to be answered on the basis of
              the following information.

   Tu Nguyen, an interior designer, received his June bank statement on July 2. The balance was $622.66. His last check stub
balance was $700. On comparing the two, he noticed that a deposit
of $275 made on January 30 was not included on the statement;
also, a bank service charge of $4 was deducted. Outstanding checks
were as follows: No. 331, $97.50; No. 332, $207; No. 335, $25.40;
and No. 336, $68.97.

8. What is Nguyen's CORRECT available bank balance?
   A. $494.79   B. $897.66   C. $700.00   D. $219.79

8.___

9. The bank statement balance referred to in the problem
   refers to the
   A. last check Tu Nguyen recorded in his checkbook
   B. last check presented for payment to Tu Nguyen's
      account
   C. amount of money left in Tu Nguyen's account according
      to the bank's calculations based on the checks,
      charges, and deposits posted to his account
   D. amount of money left in Tu Nguyen's account based
      on his own calculations of the checks, charges, and
      deposits he has written and recorded

9.___

10. What of the following endorsements would be an example of   10.___
    a simple Endorsement in Blank?
    A. Pay to the Order of Joanie Anderson
    B. Joanie Anderson
    C. For deposit only; Acct. No. 12345; Joanie Anderson
    D. Without Recourse; Joanie Anderson

11. Which of the following endorsements would limit the   11.___
    further purpose or use of the endorsed check?
    A. Pay to the Order of Joanie Anderson
    B. Joanie Anderson
    C. For deposit only; Acct. No. 12345; Joanie Anderson.
    D. Without Recourse; Joanie Anderson

12. Which of the following endorsements would protect the   12.___
    endorser from legal responsibility for payment, should
    the drawer have insufficient funds to honor his/her own
    check?
    A. Pay to the Order of Joanie Anderson
    B. Joanie Anderson
    C. For deposit only; Acct. No. 12345; Joanie Anderson
    D. Without Recourse; Joanie Anderson

Questions 13-24.

DIRECTIONS: Questions 13 - 24 are to be answered on the basis
              of the following ledger accounts for Wheelsmith
              Organic Farms.

Wheelsmith Organic Farms
Ledger Accounts

Cash	Accounts Payable	Service Supplies
1996 Jan. 1 4,000	1996 Jan. 1 2,000	1996 Jan. 1 2,000

Shelley Wheelsmith, Capital	Machinery
1996 Jan. 1 11,000	1996 Jan. 1 7,000

13. Transaction #1: On January 5, Shelley Wheelsmith, the   13.___
    proprietor, received cash amounting to $5,000 as a result
    of returning machinery that had recently been purchased.
    What account(s) should this transaction be posted to?
    A. Cash
    B. Cash and Machinery
    C. Machinery
    D. Cash, Machinery, and Service Supplies

14. Transaction #2: On January 8, Shelley Wheelsmith, the   14.___
    proprietor, sent out a check for $600 in partial payment
    of the accounts payable.
    What account(s) should this transaction be posted to?
       A. Accounts Payable
       B. Accounts Payable and Cash
       C. Accounts Payable and Capital
       D. Cash

15. Transaction #3: On January 14, Shelley Wheelsmith,   15.___
    proprietor, made an additional investment in the business
    by contributing machinery valued at $1,500.
    What account(s) should this transaction be posted to?
       A. Machinery   B. Machinery and Capital
       C. Capital   D. Machinery and Cash

16. Transaction #4: On January 26, Shelley Wheelsmith,   16.___
    proprietor, purchased additional service supplies for
    $200. She agreed to pay the obligation in 30 days.
    What account(s) should this transaction be posted to?
       A. Accounts Payable and Liabilities
       B. Service supplies
       C. Accounts Payable
       D. Accounts Payable and Service supplies

17. Transaction #5: On January 31, Shelley Wheelsmith,   17.___
    proprietor, purchased service supplies paying cash of $50.
    What account(s) should this transaction be posted to?
       A. Service supplies
       B. Service supplies and Accounts Payable
       C. Cash and Service supplies
       D. Cash

18. What is the balance in the Cash account after all of these 18.___
    transactions are posted?
       A. $9,000   B. $1,000   C. $5,000   D. $8,350

19. What is the balance in the Machinery account after all of   19.___
    these transactions are posted?
       A. $7,000   B. $5,000   C. $3,500   D. $13,500

20. What is the balance in the Accounts Payable account after   20.___
    all of these transactions are posted?
       A. $800   B. $600   C. $2,600   D. $1,600

21. What is the balance in the Capital account after all of   21.___
    these transactions are posted?
       A. $12,500   B. $800   C. $11,600   D. $10,400

22. What is the balance in the Service supplies account after   22.___
    all of these transactions are posted?
       A. $2,000   B. $2,250   C. $750   D. $2,200

23. What are the total assets of Wheelsmith Organic Farms   23.___
    after these transactions have been posted?
       A. $10,600   B. $11,850   C. $14,100   D. $10,750

24. What are the total liabilities and capital for Wheelsmith   24.___
    Organic Farms after these transactions have been posted?
       A. $14,100   B. $12,500   C. $11,850   D. $10,600

Questions 25-28.

DIRECTIONS: Questions 25 through 28 are to be answered on the
             basis of the following information.

     At the end of an accounting period, Andy's Framing Gallery
recorded the following information: Sales, $125,225; Merchandise
Inventory, December 31, 1995, $95,325; Purchases Returns and
Allowances, $3,500; Merchandise Inventory, January 1, 1996,
$98,725; Freight on Purchases, $2,500; Purchases, $120,000.

25. What are the net purchases for Andy's Framing Gallery   25.___
    during the accounting period?
       A. $120,000   B. $119,000   C. $3,500   D. $122,500

26. What is the cost of goods available for sale?   26.___
       A. $119,000   B. $98,725   C. $95,325   D. $217,725

27. What is the total cost of goods sold for this accounting   27.___
    period?
       A. $217,725   B. $95,325   C. $122,400   D. $125,225

28. What is the gross profit on sales for this accounting   28.___
    period?
       A. $2825   B. $2500   C. $125,225   D. $122,400

Questions 29-40.

DIRECTIONS: Questions 29 through 40 are to be answered on the
             basis of the following information.

     The Joie de Vivre Co. received the promissory notes listed
below during the last quarter of its calendar year:

	Date	Face Amount	Terms	Interest Rate	Date Discounted	Discount Rate
(1)	10/8	$3,600	30 days	-	10/18	9%
(2)	9/22	$8,000	60 days	6%	10/1	7%
(3)	11/15	$3,000	90 days	7%	11/20	8%

29. What is the due date for the first note?   29.___
       A. 12/31   B. 11/7   C. 12/7   D. 10/31

30. What interest will be due when the first note matures?
    A. $3   B. $3,600   C. $30   D. $0

31. What is the maturity value of the first note?
    A. $3,600   B. $3,630   C. $0   D. $3,603

32. What is the discount period for the first note?
    A. One fiscal year   B. 10 days
    C. 20 days   D. One month

33. What is the due date for the second note?
    A. 12/21   B. 11/21   C. 10/21   D. 1/21

34. What interest will be due when the second note matures?
    A. $60   B. $800.00   C. $8.00   D. $80.00

35. What is the maturity value of the second note?
    A. $8,000   B. $8,080   C. $8,800   D. $8,008

36. What is the discount period for the second note?
    A. 51 days   B. 10 days   C. 360 days   D. 60 days

37. What is the due date for the third note?
    A. 1/14   B. 12/15   C. 12/31   D. 2/13

38. What interest will be due when the third note matures?
    A. $5.25   B. $52.50   C. $525   D. $90

39. What is the maturity value of the third note?
    A. $3525   B. $3005.25   C. $3052.50   D. $3090

40. What is the discount period for the third note?
    A. 60 days   B. 85 days   C. 5 days   D. 90 days

KEY (CORRECT ANSWERS)

1. C	11. C	21. A	31. A
2. A	12. D	22. B	32. C
3. B	13. B	23. C	33. B
4. D	14. B	24. A	34. D
5. C	15. B	25. B	35. B
6. D	16. D	26. D	36. A
7. B	17. C	27. C	37. D
8. A	18. D	28. A	38. B
9. C	19. C	29. B	39. C
10. B	20. D	30. D	40. B

TEST 3

DIRECTIONS: Each question or incomplete statement is followed by
several suggested answers or completions. Select the
one that BEST answers the question or completes the
statement. *PRINT THE LETTER OF THE CORRECT ANSWER IN
THE SPACE AT THE RIGHT.*

Questions 1-8.

DIRECTIONS: Questions 1 through 8 are to be answered on the basis
of the following Balance Sheet.

Laura Lee's Bridal Shop
Balance Sheet
December 31, 1995

Assets

Cash	$14,000	
Accounts Receivable	3,000	
Bridal Accessories	10,000	
Gowns and Other Inventory	30,000	
Total Assets		$57,000

Liabilities and Capital

Accounts Payable	$ 4,000	
Notes Payable	28,000	
Total Liabilities		$32,000
Laura Lee, Capital		25,000
Total Liabilities and Capital		$57,000

1. When was the balance sheet prepared?   1.___
      A. January 1996
      B. December 31, 1995
      C. After the close of the 1995 fiscal year
      D. December 1, 1995

2. How does the date on this balance sheet differ from the   2.___
    date on the statement of capital or income statement?
      A. It doesn't differ. The dates for each statement
         signify the same time period.
      B. The date on a balance sheet represents the period
         during which any changes indicated on the statement
         took place, whereas the other financial statements
         represent the moment in time when the statement was
         prepared.
      C. The date on a balance sheet represents the moment in
         time when the statement was prepared, whereas the
         other financial statements represent the period during
         which any changes indicated on the statement took
         place.

D. The date on a balance sheet indicates an entire year, whereas the dates on the other statements indicate a single month.

3. Can Laura Lee purchase more bridal gowns for the business paying cash of $16,000?   3.__
    A. *No*, because the business has only $14,000 cash available
    B. *Yes*, because the business has $57,000 cash available
    C. *Yes*, because the business has $57,000 available in assets
    D. *No*, because the business has $57,000 in liabilities

4. What is the total equity of Laura Lee's Bridal Shop? Since total equity consists of total _____ total equity is _____.   4.__
    A. assets minus total liabilities and proprietor's capital,; $0
    B. assets minus total liabilities,; $25,000
    C. assets,; $57,000
    D. liabilities and proprietor's capital,; $57,000

5. What is the TOTAL amount of Laura Lee's claim against the total assets of the business?   5.__
    A. $57,000   B. $25,000   C. $0   D. $39,000

6. What is the amount of the creditors' claims against the assets of the business?   6.__
    A. $4,000   B. $57,000   C. $32,000   D. $28,000

7. What is the net income for the period?   7.__
    A. $57,000
    B. $0
    C. $25,000
    D. This information cannot be obtained from the balance sheet

8. What was the value of Laura Lee's ownership in this business on January 1, 1994?   8.__
    A. $25,000
    B. $57,000
    C. $14,000
    D. This information cannot be obtained from the balance sheet

Questions 9-21.

DIRECTIONS: Each of the transactions described in Questions 9 through 21 occurred within an accounting period. For each question, indicate which of the four journals the transaction would be recorded in.

9. Sale of goods on account   9.___
    A. Cash receipts   B. Cash payments
    C. General   D. Sales

10. Cash payment of a promissory note   10.___
    A. Cash payments   B. Cash receipts
    C. Sales   D. General

11. Received a credit memo from a creditor   11.___
    A. Purchases   B. General
    C. Sales   D. Cash payments

12. Sale of merchandise for cash   12.___
    A. Purchases   B. General
    C. Cash receipts   D. Cash payments

13. Received a check from a customer in partial payment of   13.___
    an oral agreement
    A. Purchases   B. Sales
    C. General   D. Cash receipts

14. Issued a credit memo to a customer   14.___
    A. Purchases   B. General
    C. Cash payments   D. Sales

15. Received a promissory note in place of an oral agreement   15.___
    from a customer
    A. General   B. Cash payments
    C. Cash receipts   D. Sales

16. Paid monthly rent   16.___
    A. General   B. Purchases
    C. Cash payments   D. Cash receipts

17. Sale of a service on credit   17.___
    A. Cash receipts   B. General
    C. Purchases   D. Sales

18. Purchase of office furniture on credit   18.___
    A. General   B. Purchases
    C. Cash payments   D. Cash receipts

19. Purchased merchandise for cash   19.___
    A. Cash payments   B. Cash receipts
    C. Sales   D. General

20. Cash refund to a customer   20.___
    A. Cash receipts   B. Sales
    C. General   D. Cash payments

21. Purchases made on credit   21.___
    A. Purchases   B. Sales
    C. Cash receipts   D. General

Questions 22-26.

DIRECTIONS: Questions 22 through 26 are to be answered on the
              basis of the following inventory, purchased by
              International Soap and Candle Traders, Inc.

700 units at $4.50, 320 units at $3.75, 550 units at $2.75,
and 475 units at $1.90

22. Calculate the total price of the units that cost $4.50.   22.___
    A. $315   B. $31,500   C. $3,150   D. $2,800

23. Calculate the total price of the units that cost $3.75.   23.___
    A. $2062.50   B. $12,000   C. $120   D. $1,200

24. Calculate the total price of the units that cost $2.75.   24.___
    A. $1,512.50   B. $15,125   C. $151.25   D. $550

25. Calculate the total price of the units that cost $1.90.   25.___
    A. $90.25   B. $9025   C. $902.50   D. $475

26. Calculate the average cost per unit.   26.___
    A. $27   B. $33.10   C. $0.30   D. $3.31

27. The interest on a promissory note is recorded at which   27.___
    of the following times?
    A. When the debt is incurred
    B. At the end of the accounting period
    C. When the note is paid
    D. At the beginning of each month

28. The interest on a promissory note begins accruing at   28.___
    which of the following times?
    A. When the debt is incurred
    B. At the end of the accounting period
    C. When the note is paid
    D. At the beginning of each month

29. The maturity value of an interest-bearing note is the   29.___
    A. interest accrued on the note plus a service charge
       imposed by the lender
    B. interest accrued on the note
    C. face value of the note
    D. principal of the note plus interest

30. A cash receipts journal is used to record the   30.___
    A. number of cash sales a business makes
    B. number of credit sales a business makes
    C. collection of cash made by the business
    D. expenditure of cash made by the business

31. Calculate the interest on a promissory note issued for
    $3,000 at an interest rate of 8%, due in 360 days.
    (Assume a banking year of 360 days.)
    A. $300   B. $240   C. $60   D. $360   31.___

32. Calculate the total payment due for a promissory note
    issued for $1,000 at an interest rate of 10%, due in
    90 days. (Assume a banking year of 360 days.)
    A. $25   B. $1050   C. $1000   D. $1025   32.___

33. Calculate the total payment due for a promissory note
    issued for $5,000 at an interest rate of 6%, due in 60
    days. (Assume a banking year of 360 days.)
    A. $5,050   B. $50   C. $5,000   D. $5,300   33.___

34. Calculate the interest on a promissory note issued for
    $1,700 at an interest rate of 12%, due in 45 days.
    (Assume a banking year of 360 days.)
    A. $204   B. $1725.50   C. $25.50   D. $1904   34.___

35. Calculate the interest on a promissory note issued for
    $600 at an interest rate of 9%, due in 90 days. (Assume
    a banking year of 360 days.)
    A. $13.50   B. $135   C. $54   D. $540   35.___

KEY (CORRECT ANSWERS)

1. B	11. B	21. A	31. B
2. C	12. C	22. C	32. D
3. A	13. D	23. D	33. A
4. D	14. B	24. A	34. C
5. B	15. A	25. C	35. A
6. C	16. C	26. D	
7. D	17. D	27. C	
8. D	18. B	28. A	
9. D	19. A	29. D	
10. A	20. D	30. C	

ARITHMETIC

EXAMINATION SECTION

DIRECTIONS FOR THIS SECTION:
Each question or incomplete statement is followed by several suggested answers or completions. Select the one that *BEST* answers the question or completes the statement. *PRINT THE LETTER OF THE CORRECT ANSWER IN THE SPACE AT THE RIGHT.*

TEST 1

1. Add $4.34, $34.50, $6.00, $101.76, $90.67. From the result, subtract $60.54 and $10.56.
   A. $76.17   B. $156.37   C. $166.17   D. $300.37   1. ...

2. Add 2,200, 2,600, 252 and 47.96. From the result, subtract 202.70, 1,200, 2,150 and 434.43.
   A. 1,112.83   B. 1,213.46   C. 1,341.51   D. 1,348.91   2. ...

3. Multiply 1850 by .05 and multiply 3300 by .08 and, then, add both results.
   A. 242.50   B. 264.00   C. 333.25   D. 356.50   3. ...

4. Multiply 312.77 by .04. Round off the result to the nearest hundredth.
   A. 12.52   B. 12.511   C. 12.518   D. 12.51   4. ...

5. Add 362.05, 91.13, 347.81 and 17.46 and then divide the result by 6. The answer, rounded off to the nearest hundredth, is:
   A. 138.409   B. 137.409   C. 136.41   D. 136.40   5. ...

6. Add 66.25 and 15.06 and, then, multiply the result by 2 1/6. The answer is, most nearly,
   A. 176.18   B. 176.17   C. 162.66   D. 162.62   6. ...

7. Each of the following items contains three decimals. In which case do all three decimals have the *SAME* value?   7. ...
   A. .3; .30; .03   B. .25; .250; .2500
   C. 1.9; 1.90; 1.09   D. .35; .350; .035

8. Add 1/2 the sum of (539.84 and 479.26) to 1/3 the sum of (1461.93 and 927.27). Round off the result to the nearest whole number.   8. ...
   A. 3408   B. 2899   C. 1816   D. 1306

9. Multiply $5,906.09 by 15% and, then, divide the result by 3 and round off to the nearest cent.   9. ...
   A. $295.30   B. $885.91   C. $2,657.74   D. $29,530.45

10. Multiply 630 by 517.   10. ...
    A. 325,710   B. 345,720   C. 362,425   D. 385,660

11. Multiply 35 by 846.   11. ...
    A. 4050   B. 9450   C. 18740   D. 29610

12. Multiply 823 by 0.05.   12. ...
    A. 0.4115   B. 4.115   C. 41.15   D. 411.50

13. Multiply 1690 by 0.10.   13. ...
    A. 0.169   B. 1.69   C. 16.90   D. 169.0

14. Divide 2765 by 35.   14. ...
    A. 71   B. 79   C. 87   D. 93

15. From $18.55 subtract $6.80.   15. ...
    A. $9.75   B. $10.95   C. $11.75   D. $25.35

16. The sum of 2.75 + 4.50 + 3.60 is: 16. ...
    A. 9.75   B. 10.85   C. 11.15   D. 11.95

17. The sum of 9.63 + 11.21 + 17.25 is: 17. ...
    A. 36.09   B. 38.09   C. 39.92   D. 41.22

18. The sum of 112.0 + 16.9 + 3.84 is: 18. ...
    A. 129.3   B. 132.74   C. 136.48   D. 167.3

19. When 65 is added to the result of 14 multiplied by 13, the   19. ...
    answer is:
    A. 92   B. 182   C. 247   D. 16055
20. From $391.55 subtract $273.45.   20. ...
    A. $118.10   B. $128.20   C. $178.10   D. $218.20

TEST 2

1. The sum of $29.61 + $101.53 + $943.64 is: 1. ...
   A. $983.88   B. $1074.78   C. $1174.98   D. $1341.42
2. The sum of $132.25 + $85.63 + $7056.44 is: 2. ...
   A. $1694.19   B. $7274.32   C. $8464.57   D. $9346.22
3. The sum of 4010 + 1271 + 838 + 23 is: 3. ...
   A. 6142   B. 6162   C. 6242   D. 6362
4. The sum of 53632 + 27403 + 98765 + 75424 is: 4. ...
   A. 19214   B. 215214   C. 235224   D. 255224
5. The sum of 76342 + 49050 + 21206 + 59989 is: 5. ...
   A. 196586   B. 206087   C. 206587   D. 234487
6. The sum of $452.13 + $963.45 + $621.25 is: 6. ...
   A. $1936.83   B. $2036.83   C. $2095.73   D. $2135.73
7. The sum of 36392 + 42156 + 98765 is: 7. ...
   A. 167214   B. 177203   C. 177313   D. 178213
8. The sum of 40125 + 87123 + 24689 is: 8. ...
   A. 141827   B. 151827   C. 151937   D. 161947
9. The sum of 2379 + 4015 + 6521 + 9986 is: 9. ...
   A. 22901   B. 22819   C. 21801   D. 21791
10. From 50962 subtract 36197.   10. ...
    A. 14675   B. 14765   C. 14865   D. 24765
11. From 90000 subtract 31928.   11. ...
    A. 58072   B. 59062   C. 68172   D. 69182
12. From 63764 subtract 21548.   12. ...
    A. 42216   B. 43122   C. 45126   D. 85312
13. From $9605.13 subtract $2715.96.   13. ...
    A. $12,321.09 B. $8,690.16   C. $6,990.07   D. $6,889.17
14. From 76421 subtract 73101.   14. ...
    A. 3642   B. 3540   C. 3320   D. 3242
15. From $8.25 subtract $6.50.   15. ...
    A. $1.25   B. $1.50   C. $1.75   D. $2.25
16. Multiply 583 by 0.50.   16. ...
    A. $291.50   B. 28.15   C. 2.815   D. 0.2815
17. Multiply 0.35 by 1045.   17. ...
    A. 0.36575   B. 3.6575   C. 36.575   D. 365.75
18. Multiply 25 by 2513.   18. ...
    A. 62825   B. 62725   C. 60825   D. 52825
19. Multiply 423 by 0.01.   19. ...
    A. 0.0423   B. 0.423   C. 4.23   D. 42.3
20. Multiply 6.70 by 3.2.   20. ...
    A. 2.1440   B. 21.440   C. 214.40   D. 2144.0

TEST 3

Questions 1-4.
DIRECTIONS: For each of Questions 1-4, perform the indicated arithmetic and choose the correct answer from among the four choices given

1. 12,485
   +   347
      A. 12,038   B. 12,128   C. 12,782   D. 12,832   1. ...

2. 74,137
   +   711
      A. 74,326   B. 74,848   C. 78,028   D. 78,926   2. ...

3. 3,749
   -   671
      A. 3,078   B. 3,168   C. 4,028   D. 4,420   3. ...

4. 19,805
   -18,904
      A. 109   B. 901   C. 1,109   D. 1,901   4. ...

5. When 119 is subtracted from the sum of 2016 + 1634, the   5. ...
   remainder is:
      A. 2460   B. 3531   C. 3650   D. 3769

6. Multiply 35 X 65 X 15.   6. ...
      A. 2275   B. 24265   C. 31145   D. 34125

7. 90% expressed as a decimal is: 7. ...
      A. .009   B. .09   C. .9   D. 9.0

8. Seven-tenths of a foot expressed in inches is: 8. ...
      A. 5.5   B. 6.5   C. 7   D. 8.4

9. If 95 men were divided into crews of five men each, the   9. ...
   number of crews that will be formed is:
      A. 16   B. 17   C. 18   D. 19

10. If a man earns $19.50 an hour, the *number* of working hours   10. ...
    it will take him to earn $4,875 is, most nearly,
       A. 225   B. 250   C. 275   D. 300

11. If 5½ loads of gravel cost $55.00, then 6½ loads will   11. ...
    cost:
       A. $60.   B. $62.50   C. $65.   D. $66.00

12. At $2.50 a yard, 27 yards of concrete will cost: 12. ...
       A. $36.   B. $41.80   C. $54.   D. $67.50

13. A distance is measured and found to be 52.23 feet. In   13. ...
    feet and inches, this distance is, most nearly, 52 feet
    and
       A. 2 3/4"   B. 3 1/4"   C. 3 3/4"   D. 4 1/4"

14. If a maintainer gets $5.20 per hour and time and one-half   14. ...
    for working over 40 hours, his *gross* salary for a week in
    which he worked 43 hours would be
       A. $208.00   B. $223.60   C. $231.40   D. $335.40

15. The circumference of a circle is given by the formula   15. ...
    C = ΠD, where C is the circumference, D is the diameter,
    and Π is about 3 1/7.
    If a coil is 15 turns of steel cable has an average diameter
    of 20 inches, the *total* length of cable on the coil is
    nearest to
       A. 5 feet   B. 78 feet   C. 550 feet   D. 943 feet

16. The measurements of a poured concrete foundation show   16. ...
    that 54 cubic feet of concrete have been placed.
    If payment for this concrete is to be on the basis of
    cubic yards, the 54 cubic feet must be
       A. multiplied by 27   B. multiplied by 3
       C. divided by 27   D. divided by 3

17. If the cost of 4 1/2 tons of structural steel is $1,800,   17. ...
    then the cost of 12 tons is, most nearly,
       A. $4,800   B. $5,400   C. $7,200   D. $216,000
18. An hourly-paid employee working 12:00 midnight to 8:00   18. ...
    a.m. is directed to report to the medical staff for a
    physical examination at 11:00 a.m. of the same day.
    The pay allowed him for reporting will be an extra
       A. 1 hour   B. 2 hours   C. 3 hours   D. 4 hours
19. The *total* length of four pieces of 2" pipe, whose lengths   19. ...
    are 7' 3½", 4' 2 3/16", 5' 7 5/16", and 8' 5 7/8", re-
    spectively, is:
       A. 24' 6 3/4"   B. 24' 7 15/16"
       C. 25' 5 13/16"   D. 25' 6 7/8"
20. As a senior mortuary caretaker, you are preparing a month-   20. ...
    ly report, using the following figures:
No. of bodies received	983
No. of bodies claimed	720
No. of bodies sent to city cemetery	14
No. of bodies sent to medical schools	9

    How many bodies remained at the end of the monthly report-
    ing period?
       A. 230   B. 240   C. 250   D. 260

KEYS (CORRECT ANSWERS)

TEST 1			TEST 2			TEST 3	
1. C	11. D		1. B	11. A		1. D	11. C
2. A	12. C		2. B	12. A		2. B	12. D
3. D	13. D		3. A	13. D		3. A	13. A
4. D	14. B		4. D	14. C		4. B	14. C
5. C	15. C		5. C	15. C		5. B	15. B
6. B	16. B		6. B	16. A		6. D	16. C
7. B	17. B		7. C	17. D		7. C	17. A
8. D	18. B		8. C	18. A		8. D	18. C
9. C	19. C		9. A	19. C		9. D	19. D
10. A	20. A		10. B	20. B		10. B	20. B

SOLUTIONS TO PROBLEMS
TEST 1

1. ($4.34 + $34.50 + $6.00 + $101.76 + $90.67) − ($60.54 + $10.56)
    = $237.27 − $71.10 = $166.17.

2. (2200 + 2600 + 252 + 47.96) − (202.70 + 1200 + 2150 + 434.43)
    = 5099.96 − 3987.13 = 1112.83

3. (1850)(.05) + (3300)(.08) = 92.5 + 264 = 356.50

4. (312.77)(.04) = 12.5108 = 12.51 to nearest hundredth

5. (362.05 + 91.13 + 347.81 + 17.46) ÷ 6 = $136.408\overline{3}$ = 136.41
    to nearest hundredth

6. (66.25 + 15.06)($2\frac{1}{6}$) = $176.171\overline{6}$ ≈ 176.17

7. .25 = .250 = .2500

8. ($\frac{1}{2}$)(539.84 + 479.26) + $\frac{1}{3}$(1461.93 + 927.27) = 509.55 + 796.4
    = 1305.95 = 1306 nearest whole number

9. ($5906.09)(.15) ÷ 3 = ($885.9135)/3 = 295.3045 = $295.30
    to nearest cent

10. (630)(517) = 325,710

11. (35)(846) = 29,610

12. (823)(.05) = 41.15

13. (1690)(.10) = 169.0

14. 2765 ÷ 35 = 79

15. $18.55 − $6.80 = $11.75

16. 2.75 + 4.50 + 3.60 = 10.85

17. 9.63 + 11.21 + 17.25 = 38.09

18. 112.0 + 16.9 + 3.84 = 132.74

19. 65 + (14)(13) = 65 + 182 = 247

20. $391.55 − $273.45 = $118.10

───

SOLUTIONS TO PROBLEMS
TEST 2

1. $29.61 + $101.53 + $943.64 = $1074.78

2. $132.25 + $85.63 + $7056.44 = $7274.32

3. 4010 + 1271 + 838 + 23 = 6142

4. 53,632 + 27,403 + 98,765 + 75,424 = 255,224

5. 76,342 + 49,050 + 21,206 + 59,989 = 206,587

6. $452.13 + $963.45 + $621.25 = $2036.83

7. 36,392 + 42,156 + 98,765 = 177,313

8. 40,125 + 87,123 + 24,689 = 151,937

9. 2379 + 4015 + 6521 + 9986 = 22,901

10. 50962 - 36197 = 14,765

11. 90,000 - 31,928 = 58,072

12. 63,764 - 21,548 = 42,216

13. $9605.13 - $2715.96 = $6889.17

14. 76,421 - 73,101 = 3320

15. $8.25 - $6.50 = $1.75

16. (583)(.50) = 291.50

17. (.35)(1045) = 365.75

18. (25)(2513) = 62,825

19. (423)(.01) = 4.23

20. (6.70)(3.2) = 21.44

SOLUTIONS TO PROBLEMS
TEST 3

1. $12,485 + 347 = 12,832$

2. $74,137 + 711 = 74,848$

3. $3749 - 671 = 3078$

4. $19,805 - 18,904 = 901$

5. $(2016 + 1634) - 119 = 3650 - 119 = 3531$

6. $(35)(65)(15) = 34,125$

7. $90\% = .90$ or $.9$

8. $(\frac{7}{10})(12) = 8.4$ inches

9. $95 \div 5 = 19$ crews

10. $\$4875 \div \$19.50 = 250$ days

11. Let x = cost. Then, $\frac{5\frac{1}{2}}{6\frac{1}{2}} = \frac{\$55.00}{x}$. $5\frac{1}{2}x = 357.50$. Solving, $x = \$65$

12. $(\$2.50)(27) = \$67.50$

13. $.23$ ft. $= 2.76$ in., so 52.23 ft ≈ 52 ft. $2\frac{3}{4}$ in. ($.76 \approx \frac{3}{4}$)

14. Salary $= (\$5.20)(40) + (\$7.80)(3) = \$231.40$

15. Length $\approx (15)(3\frac{1}{7})(20) \approx 943$ in. ≈ 78 ft.

16. There are 27 cu.ft. in 1 cu.yd. To change from 54 cu.ft. to cu.yds., divide by 27.

17. $\$1800 \div 4\frac{1}{2} = \$400$ per ton. Then, 12 tons cost $(\$400)(12) = \$4800$

18. Instead of working 12 to 8, he will be staying until 11 AM, an extra 3 hours.

19. $7'3\frac{1}{2}" + 4'2\frac{3}{16}" + 5'7\frac{5}{16}" + 8'5\frac{7}{8}" = 24'17\frac{30}{16}" = 24'18\frac{7}{8}"$

20. $983 - 720 - 14 - 9 = 240$ bodies left.

———

ARITHMETICAL REASONING
EXAMINATION SECTION

DIRECTIONS: Briefly and concisely, solve each of the following
problems using the processes of arithmetic ONLY.

1.   Successive discounts of 20% and 10% are equivalent to ____%.

Rules for Successive Discounts
  1. Express percentages as decimals.
  2. Subtract each discount from one.
  3. Multiply all the results.
  4. Subtract the product from one.

SOLUTION

Step 1. .2, .1
Step 2. .8, .9
Step 3. .8
        × .9
        ‾‾‾‾
         .72

Step 4. 1.00
       − .72
       ‾‾‾‾‾‾
         .28 = 28%   ANSWER

2.   Successive discounts of 20%, 20%, and 10% are equivalent to
____%.

SOLUTION

Step 1. .2, .2, .1
Step 2. .8, .8, .9
Step 3. .8 × .8 = .64
         .64 × .9 = .576
Step 4. 1.000
        − .576
        ‾‾‾‾‾‾‾
          .424 = 42%   ANSWER

3.   As compared with discounts of 20% and 5%, a single discount
of 25% on $600 saves ____.

SOLUTION

Part 1 - Step 1.   .2, .05
         Step 2.   .8, .95
         Step 3.   .8 × .95 = .760
         Step 4. 1.00
                 − .76
                 ‾‾‾‾‾‾
                   .24 = 24%

Part 2 - (a) .25   (b) $600
             − .24   × .01
             ‾‾‾‾‾   ‾‾‾‾‾‾‾
              .01 $6.00   ANSWER

4. The single commercial discount which is equivalent to successive discounts of 10%, 10% is ____%.

SOLUTION

Step 1.   .1, .1
Step 2.   .9, .9
Step 3.   .9 × .9 = .81
Step 4.   1.00
         - .81
          .19 = 19%   ANSWER

5. If 1/3 of the liquid contents of a can evaporated on the first day and 1/4 of the remainder on the second day, the fractional part of the original contents remaining at the close of the second day is ____.

SOLUTION

Remainder at the end of the 1st day = 2/3 (3/3 - 1/3)
1/4 × 2/3 = 2/12 = 1/6 = 1/6 evaporated on 2nd day. 2/3
(4/6)-1/6 = 3/6 = 1/2 remainder at end of 2nd day.   ANSWER

6. If an article is purchased for $7.50 and sold for $10.00, the percent of profit on the cost is ____%.

SOLUTION

C = $7.50
S.P. = $10.00
Profit = 2.50

$\frac{2.50}{7.50} = \frac{1}{3} = 33\frac{1}{3}\%$ ANSWER

7. Chairs cost $22.50 each. What must they be sold for apiece to make a profit of 40% on the selling price?

SOLUTION

Selling Price - Cost = Profit
   x = Selling Price
   x - $22.50 = .40x
   1x - .4x = 22.50
   .6x = 22.50
    x = $37.50   ANSWER

3

8. A profit of 20% on the selling price is the same as a profit of ____% on the cost.

Selling price = Cost + Profit
Let us assume:
   Selling Price = $100
   Cost   =   80
   Profit   =   20

$20 profit on the Selling Price ($100) = 20%

$$\frac{\$20 \ (P)}{\$80 \ (C)} = \frac{1}{4} = 25\% \text{ on the Cost} \quad \text{ANSWER}$$

9. A stationer purchases index cards at $1 per M. He sells them at the rate of 15¢ per C. His rate of gain on the purchase price is ____%.

Cost = $1 per M (or 10¢ per C)
Selling Price = 15¢ per C
Gain on the purchase price = 5¢
Rate of gain on purchase price $\frac{5¢}{10¢}$ = 50%   ANSWER

10. Pencils are purchased at $3 a gross and sold at 6 for 25¢. The rate of profit based on the selling price is ____%.

1 dozen sells for 50¢ (6 for 25¢ or 12 for 50¢)
A gross (twelve dozens) sells for 12 × .50 = $6
Selling Price = $6
Cost   = $3 (given)
Profit   = $3

$$\frac{\$3 \ (P)}{\$6 \ (SP)} = 50\% \quad \text{ANSWER}$$

11. Pieces of wire are soldered together so as to form the edges of a cube whose volume is 64 cubic inches. The number of inches of wire used is ____.

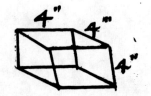

6 faces   The cube root of 64 is 4.

12 edges   12 × 4 = 48 inches   ANSWER

3

12. A bike was purchased for $50 payable in 60 days, OR at a discount of 5% cash. If a purchaser pays in 60 days, he is paying interest per annum at a rate of approximately ____%.

SOLUTION

Cost = $47.50
Interest =   2.50
Rate of interest = $\dfrac{\text{interest}}{\text{cost}}$

$\dfrac{2.50}{47.50} = \dfrac{1}{19}$ Rate for 60 days

$\dfrac{360}{60} = 6$

$\dfrac{1}{19} \times 6 = \dfrac{6}{19}$

$$\begin{array}{r} .32 \\ 19)\overline{6.00} \\ \underline{5\ 7} \\ 30 \end{array}$$

Approximately 32%   ANSWER

13. At the rate of 34¢ per $100 per year, the insurance for a three-year policy having the value of $6500 is ____.

SOLUTION

34¢ per 100
65   100's

$$\begin{array}{r} .34 \\ \times\ 65 \\ \hline \$22.10 \end{array}$$

$$\begin{array}{r} \$22.10 \\ \times\ \ 3 \\ \hline \$66.30 \end{array}$$ ANSWER

14. If the cost of living index goes up to 150 in terms of 1977, in order to retain the same purchasing power, salaries should go up to ____%.
Rule: % increase = new - old ÷ old.

SOLUTION

150 - 100 = 50
50 ÷ 100 = 1/2 = 50%   ANSWER

15. At four o'clock, the smaller angle between the hands is ____°.

SOLUTION

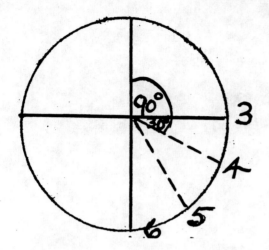

90° + 30° = 120°   ANSWER

16. A 15-gallon mixture of alcohol and water is 20% strong. If it is diluted with 5 gallons of water, its strength becomes ____%.

SOLUTION

	Old	+	Add	=	New
water	12		5	=	17
alcohol	3		0	=	3
total	15		5	=	20

$\frac{3}{20}$ = 20)$\overline{3.00}$ (.15) = 15%   ANSWER

17. The radius of a circle is multiplied by 4.
    Its area is increased by ____.

SOLUTION

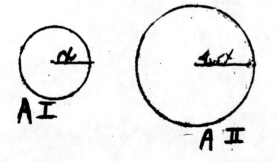

Original area = πx^2

New area   = $16\pi x^2$

A I = πx^2
A II = $\pi(4x)^2$
A II = $\pi 16x^2$ or $16\pi x^2$

The new area is 16 times that of the original area. ANSWER

18. The smaller angle between the hands of a clock at 3:30 is ___°.

SOLUTION

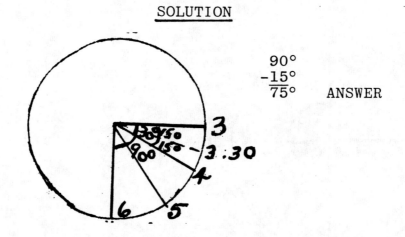

$$90°$$
$$-15°$$
$$\overline{75°} \quad \text{ANSWER}$$

19. If the radius of a circle is decreased by 5 inches, the resulting decrease in its circumference is ____ inches.

SOLUTION

$C1 = 2\pi R$
$C2 = 2\pi(R-5)$
$\quad = 2\pi R - 10\pi$
$2\pi R - (2\pi R - 10\pi) =$
$2\pi R - 2\pi R + 10\pi =$
10π (or $22/7 \times 10$)
Decrease is 10π inches.   ANSWER

20. A kilogram is approximately 2 1/5 lbs.; a cu. ft. of water weighs approximately 62 1/2 lbs. Therefore, the approximate number of kilograms in a cu. ft. of water is ____.

SOLUTION

A cu. ft. weighs $62\frac{1}{2}$ lbs.
A kilogram is 2 1/5 lbs.

$$\frac{62\ 1/2}{2\ 1/5} = \frac{125}{2} \div \frac{11}{5} = \frac{125}{2} \times \frac{5}{11} = 28 \text{ kilograms.} \quad \text{ANSWER}$$

21. A kilogram equals 35 oz. (or 1000 grams). A gram is 1/1000 of a kilogram. Find the number of grams in an ounce.

SOLUTION

A kilogram = 35 oz. (or 1000 grams)
1000 grams = 35 oz.

$$\frac{1000}{35} = 28\frac{4}{7} \text{ grams} \quad \text{ANSWER}$$

22. A meter equals 39 inches. A kilometer equals 5/8 of a mile.
Two miles is ____ kilometers.

SOLUTION

A meter = 39".
A kilometer = 5/8 of a mile
One mile is 8/5 of a kilometer
2 miles is 2 × 8/5 = 3.2 kilometers   ANSWER

23. A room 27 ft. by 32 ft. is to be carpeted. The width of the
carpet is 27 inches. The length, in yards, of the carpet
needed for this floor is ____ yards.

SOLUTION

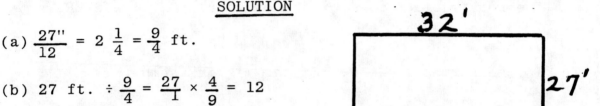

(a) $\frac{27"}{12}$ = $2\frac{1}{4}$ = $\frac{9}{4}$ ft.

(b) 27 ft. ÷ $\frac{9}{4}$ = $\frac{27}{1}$ × $\frac{4}{9}$ = 12

(c) 32 ft.
    ×12 strips
    ‾‾‾‾‾
    384 ft. ÷ 3 ft. = 128 yards   ANSWER

24. The diameter of the moon is approximately 2000 miles. The ratio
of the surface of the moon to the surface of the earth is,
therefore, approximately ____.

SOLUTION

The surface (area) of a body is proportional to the square of
its linear dimensions. (The area is proportional to the
square of its diameter.)

$\frac{A1}{A2}$ = $(\frac{2000}{8000})^2$ = $(\frac{1}{4})^2$ = $\frac{1}{16}$

$\frac{A1}{A2}$ = $(\frac{D1}{D2})^2$ ANSWER: 1:16

25. If one acute angle of a right triangle is 5 times the other,
the number of degrees in the smallest angle of the triangle
is ____.

SOLUTION

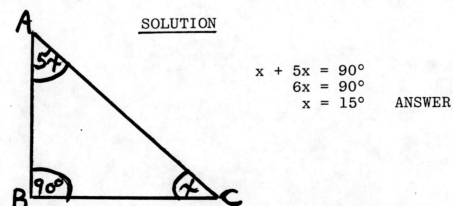

x + 5x = 90°
6x = 90°
x = 15°   ANSWER

26. Doubling the denominator of a fraction and dividing the numerator by 2 yields a fraction _____ the value of the original fraction.

SOLUTION

Let x = numerator
Let y = denominator

$\frac{x}{y}$ is the original fraction

$$\frac{x \div 2}{2y} = \frac{x}{2} \times \frac{1}{2y} = \frac{1x}{4y}$$

The new fraction is $\frac{1}{4}$ of the original ($\frac{x}{y}$).   ANSWER

27. In the series 1, 4, 9, 16, the missing number is _____.

SOLUTION

Solve in different ways

(a) Differences -- 3, 5, 7, 9 | 16 + 9 = 25   ANSWER
(b) Square Roots - 1, 2, 3, 4, 5, 6 | 5^2 = 25   ANSWER

28. A ship has a length of 1020 feet. The fractional part of a mile to which this length is equivalent is approximately _____.

SOLUTION

$\frac{1020}{5200}$ = approximately $\frac{1}{5}$ ANSWER

29. Bank A gives interest at 2½% per annum. Bank B gives interest at 2 3/4%. Interest in each case is entered quarterly. The difference in interest for a given quarter on an $800 deposit is _____.

SOLUTION

Calculate interest on $200 (¼ of $800)

```
  .025          .0275         $5.50
× 200         ×  200        - 5.00
$5.00         $5.5000          .50    ANSWER
```

30. The floor of a hall which is 3 yards wide and 20 feet long is to be covered with carpet which is 1½ yards wide. The length of carpet needed to cover the floor is _____ feet.

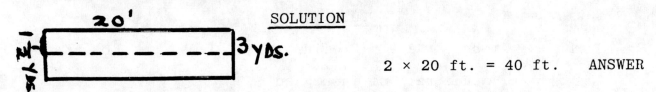

SOLUTION

2 × 20 ft. = 40 ft.   ANSWER

31. A bill in the amount of $100 is to be paid at a discount of 20%, 5%. The net amount to be paid is _____.

SOLUTION

Step 1.   .2, .05
Step 2.   .8, .95
Step 3.   .95
           ×.8
          .760

Step 4. 1.00
         -.76
          .24 = 24% (of discount)

$100
- 24 (24% × $100)
$ 76 ANSWER

32. The price of an article has been reduced 25%. In order to restore the original price, the new price must be increased by _____%.

SOLUTION

Original Price = $100 (assumed)
Reduced Price = $ 75

Problem: To find the % increase to restore the original price

Let x = rate of increase

$75 + 75x = 100; \quad 75x = 25; \quad x = \dfrac{25}{75} = \dfrac{1}{3} = 33 \ 1/3\%$ ANSWER

33. A stationer buys blankbooks at 75¢ a dozen and sells them at 25¢ apiece. The gross profit based on the cost is _____%.

SOLUTION

C = 75¢ a dozen; Selling Price = $3 a dozen (25¢ each); P = $2.25

Rate of Profit $= \dfrac{P}{C}(\dfrac{2.25}{.75}) = 3 = 300\%$ ANSWER

34. A fire insurance policy is marked as follows: Amount of insurance $3800; premium $19; period 9/1/84 to 8/31/87. This is equivalent to a per annum rate of ____ %.

SOLUTION

Formula: Amount × Rate = Premium

Let x = per annum rate of insurance

$$\frac{3800x}{1} = \frac{19}{3}$$

$$x = \frac{19}{3} \div 3800$$

$$x = \frac{19}{3} \times \frac{1}{3800} = \frac{1}{600} = \frac{1}{6}\% \quad \text{ANSWER}$$

35. A mortgage on a house in the amount of $4000 provides for quarterly payments of $200 plus interest on the unpaid balance at $4\frac{1}{2}$%. The total second payment to be made is ____.

SOLUTION

$4000 unpaid principal
- 200 1st payment
$3800 unpaid balance after 1st payment has been deducted. (You do not pay interest on the balance at this time because you have not had the use of the money.)

$4\frac{1}{2}$% for a year = 1 1/8% for a quarter of a year

```
$3800              $ 42.75
× .01 1/8          +200.00
  475              $242.75  Total amount of 2nd payment
 3800                       ANSWER
$42.75 interest
```

36. A cylindrical mailing tube whose length is 6 inches and whose diameter is $3\frac{1}{2}$ inches is unrolled. The area of the resulting rectangle in square inches is approximately ____.

SOLUTION

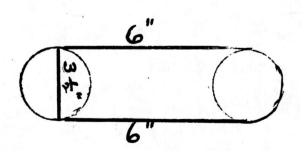

C = 2πR (or πD)

$$(\pi = \frac{22}{7} \text{ or } 3.14)$$

$$C = \frac{22}{7} \times \frac{3.5}{1} = 11$$

Area of rectangle = 1 × w

∴ 6 × 11 = 66 sq. in. ANSWER

37. If one acute angle of a right triangle is 4 times the other, the number of degrees in the smallest angle of the triangle is ____.

SOLUTION

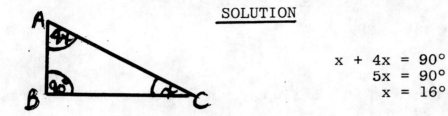

$$x + 4x = 90°$$
$$5x = 90°$$
$$x = 16° \quad \text{ANSWER}$$

38. The formula F = 9/5 C plus 32 shows that when C is increased by 10, F will increase by ____.

SOLUTION

$$F1 = \frac{9}{5} C + 32$$

$$F2 = \frac{9}{5}(C+10) + 32$$

$$= \frac{9}{5} C + \frac{90}{5} + 32$$

$$= \text{(increase is) } 18 \quad \text{ANSWER}$$

39. Canned fruit is sold in two weights - 8 oz. and 12 oz. (avoirdupois). The former sells 2 for 39¢. The latter 25¢ a can. A woman needs 6 lbs. How much will she save by buying the larger cans? ____

SOLUTION

8 oz. = ½ lb. (16 oz. in 1 lb.)
Small cans sell for 39¢ a lb. (2 cans)
The large cans (12 oz.) = 3/4 lb. at 25¢ a lb.

$$1 \text{ lb.} = \frac{4}{3} \times .25 = \frac{1.00}{3} = .33 \frac{1}{3} \quad \text{(price of 1 lb. large can)}$$

```
  39.0¢           5.7¢
 -33.3¢          × 6
  ─────          ─────
   5.7¢          34.2¢        ANSWER:   34¢
```

40. A liter of water weighs 1000 grams. A pint of water weighs a pound, and is approximately equal to a half liter. It follows, therefore, that a kilogram equals (approximately) ____ lbs.

SOLUTION

A liter weighs 1000 grams (or 1 kilogram)
A pint = 1/2 a liter (weighs 1 lb.)
        = 1 liter weighs 2 lbs.
A liter weighs 1 kilogram (1000 grams)
A kilogram weighs 2 lbs.   ANSWER

41. If a cord of wood measures 8 ft. by 4 ft. by 4 ft., the number of cords in a pile 24 ft. by 6 ft. by 4 ft. is ____ .

SOLUTION

$$\frac{24 \times 6 \times 4}{8 \times 4 \times 4} = \frac{9}{2} = 4\frac{1}{2} \quad \text{ANSWER}$$

42. To yield a return of 4%, a $1000 bond which pays 3% interest may be purchased at ____ .

SOLUTION

$1000 bond pays $30 interest
Let x = cost of a $1000 bond

.04x = $30.00 $\frac{\text{Interest}}{\text{Cost}} (\frac{30}{x}) = \frac{4}{100} = \frac{1}{25}$

  4x = $3000

   x = $750   ANSWER   x = 25 × 30 = $750   ANSWER

Proof
$750
× .04
$30.00

43. A finishes a job in $2\frac{1}{2}$ hours and B can do it in 3 1/3 hours. How long will it take both of them working together? ____ hours.

SOLUTION

Formula: Divide the product by the sum (if only 2 numbers are involved)

$$\frac{5}{2} \times \frac{10}{3} = \frac{50}{6} \qquad\qquad \frac{50}{6} \div \frac{35}{6} =$$

$$\frac{15}{6} + \frac{20}{6} = \frac{35}{6} \qquad\qquad \frac{50}{6} \times \frac{6}{35} = \frac{10}{7} = 1\frac{3}{7} \text{ hours} \quad \text{ANSWER}$$

44. X can do a job in 3 days, Y in 4 days, and Z in 6 days. If all work together, how long will it take to finish the job?

SOLUTION

In one day: X does 1/3 of the job, Y does 1/4, Z does 1/6

All together in one day: $\frac{4}{12} + \frac{3}{12} + \frac{2}{12} = \frac{9}{12} = \frac{3}{4}$

Then, $\frac{1}{\frac{3}{4}}$ (entire job) $= \frac{4}{3} = 1 \ 1/3$ days (for entire job)

45. A snapshot measures 1 7/8" by 2 1/2". It is enlarged so that the larger dimension will be 4 inches. The length of the shorter dimension will be ____ inches.

SOLUTION

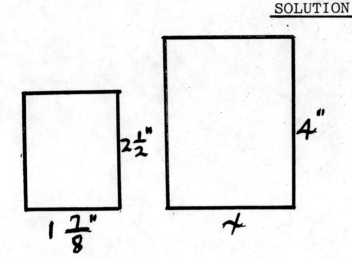

$$\frac{1\frac{7}{8}}{x} = \frac{2\frac{1}{2}}{4}$$

$$\frac{15}{8} \div x = \frac{5}{2} \div 4$$

$$\frac{15}{8} \times \frac{1}{x} = \frac{5}{2} \times \frac{1}{4}$$

$$\frac{15}{8x} \qquad \frac{5}{8}$$

$$40x = 120$$
$$x = 3 \quad \text{ANSWER}$$

46. A square figure has as many inches in its perimeter as it has square inches in its area. The length of one side of this square, in inches, is ____.

SOLUTION

Let x = the number of inches in one of the sides
4x = the perimeter
x^2 = the area

$$4x = x^2 \qquad\qquad x = 0$$
$$x^2 - 4x = 0 \qquad x-4 = 0$$
$$x(x-4) = 0 \qquad x = 4 \quad \text{ANSWER}$$

Proof:
$\overline{4 \times 4} = 4 + 4 + 4 + 4$

47. A man can exert a force of 150 lbs. He wants to use a 10-foot lever to lift a stone weighing 900 lbs. Where must he pivot the lever?

SOLUTION

Lever
  or
Fulcrum x = Distance from A to B
                $10-x$ = Distance from B to C

$$900x = 150(10-x)$$
$$900x = 1500 - 150x$$
$$1050x = 1500$$
$$x = \frac{150}{105} = 1\frac{3}{7} \quad \text{ANSWER}$$

OR

$$\frac{900}{150} = \frac{6}{1}$$

$$\therefore \frac{10-x}{x} = \frac{6}{1}$$

$$6x = 10-x$$
$$7x = 10$$
$$x = 1\frac{3}{7} \quad \text{ANSWER}$$

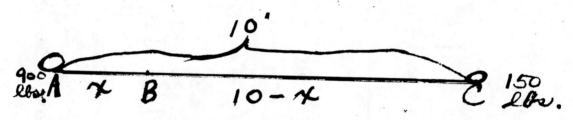

LEVER OR FULCRUM

48. Two stations, A and B, are located 6 miles apart on a railroad. The rates of cartage of coal are 50¢ per ton per mile from A, and 75¢ per ton per mile from B. At a certain consumer's home, located on the railroad between A and B, the cost for cartage is the same whether the coal is delivered from A or from B. Find the distance from this home to A. _____ miles.
   A. 5 3/5   B. 3 3/5   C. 3 4/5   D. 5 4/5

SOLUTION

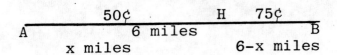

Fulcrum
   Cost = Cost

Let x = distance from home to A
   50x = cost from A to home
75(6-x) = Cost from B to home
      50x = 450 - 75x
    125x = 450
        x = 3 3/5 miles   ANSWER: (B)

49. The population of a city is approximately 7.85 millions. The area is approximately 200 square miles. The number of thousand persons per square mile is
   A. 3.925   B. 39.25   C. 392.5   D. 39250

SOLUTION
       40,000 (number of persons per square mile)
200)8,000,000 (approximate population)

ANSWER: (B) or (approximately) 40 (thousand persons per sq. mi.)

50. The longest straight line that can be drawn to connect two points on the circumference of a circle whose radius is 9 inches is _____ inches.
   A. 9   B. 18   C. 28.2753   D. 4.5

SOLUTION

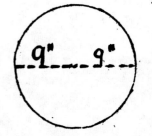

9" + 9" = 18 inches   ANSWER

EXAMINATION SECTION
TEST 1

DIRECTIONS: Each question or incomplete statement is followed by several suggested answers or completions. Select the one that BEST answers the question or completes the statement. *PRINT THE LETTER OF THE CORRECT ANSWER IN THE SPACE AT THE RIGHT.*

1. Our number system has a base of   1.___
   A. 2   B. 5   C. 10   D. 60

2. To find the average weight of the football team,   2.___
   A. add and divide
   B. multiply
   C. add
   D. divide the weight of each player

3. The thermometer used to measure the temperature of a   3.___
   school is called
   A. Centigrade   B. Fahrenheit
   C. fever thermometer   D. gauge

4. The value of a fraction is changed when the same number is   4.___
   _____ to both numerator and denominator.
   A. added   B. divided
   C. multiplied
   D. reduced to both terms of the fraction

5. Stores buy their merchandise from firms called   5.___
   A. commissioners   B. retail firms
   C. factories   D. wholesale firms

6. The amount of money you borrow is called the   6.___
   A. amount   B. discount
   C. principal   D. bank discount

7. An angle of 75° is called a(n) ____ angle.   7.___
   A. acute   B. obtuse   C. straight   D. right

8. The rate of interest could be found by the formula   8.___
   A. I = Prt   B. r = i/pt   C. r = Pt   D. I = P/Rt

9. If three sides of one triangle are equal to the three   9.___
   sides of the other, the triangles are
   A. equilateral   B. right triangles
   C. scalene   D. congruent

10. A rectangular solid could be called a(n)   10.___
    A. plane   B. irregular figure
    C. polygon   D. prism

11. A written promise to repay the face of a loan is a   11.___
    A. refund   B. promissory note
    C. dividend   D. deposit

12. The ^{2} written above the s in the formula As^2 means   12.___
    A. 2s   B. s × s   C. s + s   D. s/2

13. Selling price includes cost plus profit plus   13.___
    A. expenses   B. profit   C. loss   D. net price

14. When numbers are used to express how many or how much   14.___
of units of measure, they are called
    A. digits   B. denominate numbers
    C. integers   D. whole numbers

15. The square of a number is that number multiplied by   15.___
    A. two   B. twice the number
    C. four   D. itself

16. When the merchant permits the customer to make a down   16.___
payment and make regular payments on an article, this
form of payment is called
    A. dues   B. rent
    C. installment buying   D. utility payments

17. Circles that have a common center and different radii are   17.___
____ circles.
    A. equal   B. center   C. congruent   D. concentric

18. The United States standard of measure of length is the   18.___
    A. base 10   B. meter
    C. English system   D. metric system

19. If you put money to work for you, the income you receive   19.___
is called
    A. income taxes   B. interest
    C. bank discount   D. sales tax

20. A fraction whose numerator is a fraction and denominator   20.___
is an integer is a ____ fraction.
    A. common   B. decimal   C. improper   D. complex

KEY (CORRECT ANSWERS)

1. C		11. B	
2. A		12. B	
3. B		13. A	
4. A		14. B	
5. D		15. D	
6. C		16. C	
7. A		17. D	
8. B		18. C	
9. D		19. B	
10. D		20. D	

SOLUTIONS TO PROBLEMS

1. 10 is the base of our number system. Ex: $456 = (4)(10^2) + (5)(10) + 6$.

2. To find average weight, add and divide.

3. Fahrenheit degrees would be used for schools.

4. A fraction will change when the same number is added to both numerator and denominator. Ex: Add 5 to both parts of $\frac{2}{3}$ to get $\frac{7}{8}$, and $\frac{7}{8} \neq \frac{2}{3}$.

5. Stores buy merchandise from wholesale firms.

6. Principal = amount of money borrowed.

7. 75° is an acute angle since it is less than 90°.

8. $R = I/(PT)$ shows rate in terms of interest, principal, and time.

9. If 3 sides of one triangle match 3 sides of a second triangle, they are congruent (SSS).

10. A rectangular solid is a special kind of prism.

11. Promissory note = written promise to repay a loan.

12. $s^2 = s \times s$

13. Selling price includes cost, profit, and expenses.

14. Denominate numbers express units of measure. Ex: 8 gallons.

15. Square of any number = that number times itself.
Ex: $4^2 = 4 \times 4 = 16$

16. Installment buying = down payment + regular payments
Ex: $1000 down payment + $300 payment per month for 2 years.

17. Concentric circles have a common center but different radii. Diagram appears as:

18. The English system is the U.S. standard measure of length. This includes inches, feet, yards, miles, etc.

19. Interest = income received when money is put to work (invested).

20. A complex fraction would contain a fraction within its numerator, denominator, or both.

Ex 1: $\dfrac{\frac{1}{2}}{\frac{1}{3}} = \dfrac{1}{2} \cdot \dfrac{3}{1} = \dfrac{3}{2}$

Ex 2: $\dfrac{\frac{1}{2}}{3} = \dfrac{1}{2} \cdot \dfrac{1}{3} = \dfrac{1}{6}$

Ex 3: $\dfrac{1}{\frac{2}{3}} = \dfrac{1}{1} \cdot \dfrac{3}{2} = \dfrac{3}{2}$

TEST 2

DIRECTIONS: Each question or incomplete statement is followed by several suggested answers or completions. Select the one that BEST answers the question or completes the statement. *PRINT THE LETTER OF THE CORRECT ANSWER IN THE SPACE AT THE RIGHT.*

1. Sally is going to Chicago for a visit. The bus fare is $27.85 one way or a round-trip ticket would be $51.56. How much can Sally save by buying a round-trip ticket rather than two one-way tickets?
   A. $4.20
   C. $4.14
   B. $2.07
   D. None of the above

   1. ___

2. The Webster Junior High School collected $226.45 for Junior Red Cross and $420.55 for the Community Chest. There were 850 students in the school. To the NEAREST cent, what was the average contribution?
   A. $.76
   C. $1.00
   B. $.50
   D. None of the above

   2. ___

3. Jack borrowed $57.50 from his father and agreed to pay it in twelve monthly payments of $5.00 each. How much interest did he pay?
   A. $2.50
   C. $7.50
   B. $3.50
   D. None of the above

   3. ___

4. Joe's mother bought a roast weighing 6 3/4 lbs. at 89¢ a pound. How much change did she receive from a $10.00 bill?
   A. $3.99
   C. $6.01
   B. $5.01
   D. None of the above

   4. ___

5. The Athletic Department paid $45 total tax on 1,000 tickets. How much tax was this per ticket?
   A. $.22
   C. 4.5 cents
   B. $.45
   D. None of the above

   5. ___

6. Mary bought $4\frac{1}{2}$ yards of lace. She used 1 2/3 yards of it on a blouse. ____ yards of lace were left.
   A. 3 1/6
   C. 2 5/6
   B. $3\frac{1}{2}$
   D. None of the above

   6. ___

7. The girls are going to make aprons for Junior Red Cross. The pattern calls for 3/4 yard of material for one apron. They will need ____ yards for 25 aprons.
   A. 33 1/3
   C. 20
   B. 18 3/4
   D. None of the above

   7. ___

8. Which city on a world map of standard time zones would be NEAR the 75°W?
    A. Greenwich
    B. Sydney
    C. Calcutta
    D. None of the above

8. ___

9. John's father made a down payment on a car and has $1320 left to pay. He pays $55 each month.
It will take him ____ months to finish the car payments.
    A. 42
    B. 24
    C. 18
    D. None of the above

9. ___

10. Pete bought a board 12 ft. 8 in. long from which he wants to make three shelves. Two of the shelves are 2 ft. 8 in. long, and the third shelf is 1 ft. 6 in. long.
How long will the piece be that is left over?
    A. 5 ft. 8 in.
    B. 5 ft. 10 in.
    C. 6 ft. 10 in.
    D. None of the above

10. ___

11. A factory worker received an increase of 15% in his hourly wages. His former wages were $1.80 per hour.
How much a week did his wages INCREASE in a forty-hour week?
    A. $21.17
    B. $8.00
    C. $10.80
    D. None of the above

11. ___

12. Find the installment price of a washing machine if the down payment is $39.90, the monthly payments are $14.13 for twelve months, and the interest charge is $9.96.
    A. $179.52
    B. $219.42
    C. $169.56
    D. None of the above

12. ___

13. How many hundreds in 18762?
    A. 7
    B. 87
    C. 187
    D. None of the above

13. ___

14. The football team won 16 games and lost 4 games.
What percent of the games played did they win?
    A. 75%
    B. 80%
    C. 40%
    D. None of the above

14. ___

15. The bakery boxed doughnuts one half dozen to a box.
They will have ____ full boxes if they fry 500 doughnuts.
    A. 41
    B. 83
    C. 82
    D. None of the above

15. ___

16. Jane's parents burn fuel oil. They have used 180 gallons. The gauge indicates the tank is 5/8 full.
The tank holds ____ gallons.
    A. 255
    B. 480
    C. 600
    D. None of the above

16. ___

17. ____ tiles, each a 9" square, could be laid in one width of a recreation room that is 25 feet long and $16\frac{1}{2}$ feet wide.
    A. 22
    B. 149
    C. 51
    D. None of the above

17. ___

18. The outside diameter of a wheel on Bob's bicycle is 28   18. ___
    inches. The outside diameter of a wheel on his little
    brother's bicycle is 21 inches. After traveling a mile
    the little brother's wheel will make ___ revolutions more.
    A. 1080   B. 269.5
    C. 240   D. None of the above

19. Bill gets 17 3/4 miles per gallon.   19. ___
    At this rate, he should get ___ miles if he buys 5.6
    gallons of gasoline.
    A. 317   B. 99.4
    C. 85   D. None of the above

20. The scale drawing of a house is 1 in. = 12 ft.   20. ___
    If a room is 33 feet long, a ___ inch line should be
    used on the blueprint to represent that distance.
    A. 2 3/4   B. 3.3
    C. 2.1   D. None of the above

21. A 2-inch gear makes 75 revolutions per minute.   21. ___
    A 3-inch gear makes ___ rpm at the same rate of speed.
    A. 12½   B. 112½
    C. 50   D. None of the above

22. What is the selling price of a radio that cost the dealer   22. ___
    $36 and the margin is 40% of the selling price?
    A. $60   B. $45
    C. $50.40   D. None of the above

23. Mr. Jacks used 35 kwh.   23. ___
    If the charge is 8¢ a kwh for the first 20 kwh and 5¢ a
    kwh for the remainder, what was the TOTAL charge?
    A. $2.35   B. $3.35
    C. $4.55   D. None of the above

24. Druggists use a unit of measurement of weight called the   24. ___
    grain. There are *approximately* 437.5 grains in an ounce.
    There are APPROXIMATELY ___ grains in a pound.
    A. 7000   B. 5252
    C. 73,400   D. None of the above

25. A gasoline tank is 16 ft. high and has a diameter of   25. ___
    14 ft.
    The tank will hold ___ cubic feet of gasoline (use 22/7
    for pi) to the NEAREST 10 cu.ft.
    A. 704   B. 784
    C. 2460   D. None of the above

KEY (CORRECT ANSWERS)

1. C
2. A
3. A
4. A
5. C

6. C
7. B
8. D
9. B
10. B

11. C
12. B
13. C
14. B
15. B

16. B
17. A
18. C
19. B
20. A

21. C
22. A
23. A
24. A
25. C

SOLUTIONS TO PROBLEMS

1. Savings = ($27.85)(2) - $51.56 = $4.14

2. Average contribution = ($226.45 + $420.55) ÷ 850 = $647 ÷ 850 ≈ $.76

3. Interest = (12)($5.00) - $57.50 = $2.50

4. $10.00 - (6.75)(.89) = $3.99 change

5. $45 ÷ 1000 = .045 = 4.5 cents tax per ticket

6. $4\frac{1}{2} - 1\frac{2}{3} = 4\frac{3}{6} - 1\frac{4}{6} = 3\frac{9}{6} - 1\frac{4}{6} = 2\frac{5}{6}$ yds. left

7. $(\frac{3}{4})(25) = 18\frac{3}{4}$ yds. needed

8. Refer to world map. None is correct.

9. $1320 ÷ 55 = 24 months

10. 12'8" - 2'8" - 2'8" - 1'6" = 152" - 32" - 32" - 18" = 70"
    = 5'10"

11. Increase = ($1.80)(.15)(40) = $10.80 per week

12. $39.90 + ($14.13)(12) + $9.96 = $219.42 installment price

13. 18,762 ÷ 100 = 187 with remainder of 62. So, there are 187
    hundreds in 18,762.

14. Percent won = $\frac{16}{20}$ = 80%

15. 500 ÷ 6 = $83\frac{1}{3}$, which means 83 full boxes + $\frac{1}{3}$ of a box

16. 180 gallons represents $\frac{3}{8}$ of the entire tank. Thus, the tank's
    capacity = 180 ÷ $\frac{3}{8}$ = 480 gallons.

17. 25' = 300" and $16\frac{1}{2}$' = 198". Now, 300 ÷ 9 = $33\frac{1}{3}$ and 198 ÷ 9 = 22.
    Then the number of tiles that could fit in 1 width = 22.
    (The actual number of tiles that could fit in the entire room
    = (22)(33) = 726)

18. 1 revolution of Bob's bicycle = $2\pi r$ = $(2 \times \frac{22}{7} \times 14)$ = 88"

1 revolution of his brother's bicycle = $2\pi r$ = $(2 \times \frac{22}{7} \times 10.5)$ = 6

1 mile = 63,360"

∴ Bob's bicycle wheel will make $(\frac{63,360}{88})$ revs = 720

His brother's wheel will make $(\frac{63,360}{66})$ revs = 960

∴ His brother's wheel will make 240 revs more

19. $(17\frac{3}{4})(5.6)$ = $(17.75)(5.6)$ = 99.4 miles

20. $33 \div 12 = 2\frac{3}{4}$-inch line needed

21. Let x = rpm. $\frac{2}{3} = \frac{x}{75}$. Solving, x = 50
Note: Size of gear is inversely related to rpm.

22. Let x = selling price. Then, $36 = .60x$. Solving, x = $60

23. Total charge = $(.08)(20) + (.05)(15)$ = $2.35

24. $(437.5)(16)$ = 7000 grains in a pound (approx.)

25. Volume = $(\pi)(7^2)(16) \approx 2460$ cu.ft.

———

ARITHMETICAL REASONING
EXAMINATION SECTION
TEST 1

DIRECTIONS: Each question or incomplete statement is followed by several suggested answers or completions. Select the one that BEST answers the question or completes the statement. *PRINT THE LETTER OF THE CORRECT ANSWER IN THE SPACE AT THE RIGHT.*

1. The initial mark-up in a store is 40%; mark-downs are 5%; shortages 1%; cash discounts 5%; alteration costs .5%; expenses 25%.
    The maintained mark-up is
    A. 34%   B. 39%   C. 36.4%   D. 30%   1.___

2. A buyer of TV sets wishes to maintain a mark-up of $37\frac{1}{2}$% after all mark-downs are taken. Of 25 sets costing $150 each, he sells 20 at $265.
    How much can he mark-down the remaining 5 sets and still realize his mark-up objective?
    A. $166   B. $150   C. $140   D. $125   2.___

3. An article originally selling for $12 and costing $8 was marked down to $10. Assuming the same markup,
    what is the present market value of its cost?
    A. $6.68   B. $8.00   C. $5.67   D. $6.86   3.___

4. What is the *on* percentage of trade discounts of 20% and 10%?
    A. 70   B. 85   C. 72   D. 80   4.___

5. Canadian cost of a sweater is $40. Packing and labor cost $5.00; ad valorem duty, 40%; specific duty,65¢; rate of exchange, .9091.
    What is the duty in American currency?
    A. $16.96   B. $16.36   C. $18.00   D. $18.60   5.___

6. A bolt of cloth measures 40 yards. The following yardages are sold: $4\frac{1}{2}$, 5 3/4, 6 7/8.
    How many yards are left?
    A. 23 7/8   B. $22\frac{1}{2}$ C. 22 7/8   D. 24 3/8   6.___

7. A shirt manufacturer has $76\frac{1}{2}$ yards of broadcloth to be used for shirts.
    If each shirt takes $2\frac{1}{2}$ yards, how many shirts can he make?
    A. 38   B. 30   C. 19   D. 31   7.___

8. Subtract 1.003 from 24.5.
    A. 24.003   B. 12.42   C. 23.2   D. 23.497   8.___

9. A store carries a stock amounting to $265,830.25. Cash discounts, on the average, amount to $5\frac{1}{4}$%.
    How much are the cash discounts?
    A. $13,956.09   B. $1,395.61
    C. $139.56   D. $1.39   9.___

10. If the sales in a department totaled $67,507.50 and the average sale was $22.50, how many transactions were there?
    A. 3,000   B. 300   C. 30,000   D. 30

10.___

11. A department store reports a decrease in sales of 5.5% for this year.
If this year's sales are $275,825,000, last year's sales were
    A. $291,878,000   B. $290,995,000
    C. $260,655,000   D. $290,788,000

11.___

12. For the current year, the sales volume in a store was $50,000,000. Other income amounted to $1,500,000. Operating expenses were $10,000,000; cost of goods sold, $37,500,000.
What is the percent of net profit based on retail?
    A. 10   B. 8   C. 50   D. 13

12.___

13. If this year's sales show an increase of 300% over last year, this year's sales are how many times last year's sales?
    A. 3   B. 1 1/3   C. 4   D. $\frac{1}{4}$

13.___

14. Net sales in a shop amounted to $374,000; returns were 10%; allowances, 5%.
What were the gross sales?
    A. $430,100   B. $415,000   C. $411,400   D. $440,000

14.___

15. If the average sale in a store is expected to rise 5% over last year, and the number of transactions increases 3%, what percentage of increase in dollar sales volume should be planned?
    A. 8   B. 4   C. 8.15   D. 8.51

15.___

16. The billed cost on an invoice is $300; freight charges, $10; cash discount, 2%; the retail value of the merchandise is $525.
The mark-up percent on retail is
    A. 40.9   B. 42   C. 69   D. 69.5

16.___

17. A hat costing $30.00 is to be given a mark-up of 45% on retail.
The retail should be
    A. $43.50   B. $46.40   C. $55.40   D. $54.50

17.___

18. Retail price $40 per unit; mark-up 40% of retail; transportation charge $1 per unit.
Find billed cost that store can pay.
    A. $23   B. $24   C. $23.75   D. $24.75

18.___

19. A buyer plans to spend $17,000 at retail for merchandise   19.___
    at a mark-up of 34%. He finds a special value at $3,000
    that he can sell for $6,000.
    What mark-up percentage does he need on the balance of
    his purchases in order to achieve his planned 34%?
       A. 35   B. 19.9   C. 15   D. 22.5

20. A store has a gross margin of 40% and reductions of 13%.   20.___
    Cash discount on purchases are not credited to the
    department. There are no alteration costs.
    What is the initial mark-up?
       A. 46%   B. 53%   C. 27%   D. 26%

21. A dress is to retail for $35 with a mark-up of 40% of   21.___
    retail.
    The cost of the dress to the retailer was
       A. $25   B. $21   C. $14   D. $20

22. The cost is $1.20 and the desired gross profit is 40% of   22.___
    retail.
    The retail price should be
       A. $1.60   B. $1.68   C. $2.00   D. $2.40

23. The realized mark-up on a TV set is $50. The mark-up is   23.___
    25% of retail.
    The cost of the TV set to the retailer was
       A. $200   B. $125   C. $100   D. $150

24. Farnum, a salesman, earns $9.60 per hour for 40 hours a   24.___
    week, with time and a half for all hours over 40 per week.
    Last week, his total earnings were $470.40.
    How many hours did he work last week?
       A. 46   B. 49   C. 47   D. 48

25. Dane & Clarke, partners, share profits in a 5:3 ratio.   25.___
    Dane's share of the profit for this year was $12,000 more
    than Clarke's share.
    Clarke's share of the net profit was
       A. $30,000   B. $48,000   C. $36,000   D. $18,000

KEY (CORRECT ANSWERS)

1. C	6. C	11. A	16. A	21. B
2. D	7. B	12. B	17. D	22. C
3. A	8. D	13. C	18. A	23. D
4. C	9. A	14. D	19. B	24. A
5. A	10. A	15. C	20. A	25. D

SOLUTIONS TO PROBLEMS

1. $5 + 5 - 1 = 9\%$. Then, $(40\%)(.91) = 36.4\%$

2. $(25)(\$150) = \$3750$ and $\$3750 \div .625 = \$6000$ total selling price of all sets. $\$6000 - (20)(\$265) = \$700$; $700 \div 5 = \$140$ selling price for each of the last 5 sets. Markdown amount $= \$265 - \$140 = \$125$

3. When the article's original selling price was \$12, its cost was \$8.00. If the article's original selling price were to be \$10, it would cost $\$(\frac{8.00}{12.00} \times 10.00) = \$6.67$

4. Resulting percentage $= (1-.20)(1-.10) = .72 = 72\%$

5. $(\$45)(.40) = \$18$, $18 + .65 = \$18.65$. Then, $(\$18.65)(.9091) \approx \$16.95$, closest to \$16.96 in American currency.

6. $40 - 4\frac{1}{2} - 5\frac{3}{4} - 6\frac{7}{8} = 22\frac{7}{8}$ yds.

7. $76\frac{1}{2} \div 2\frac{1}{2} = 30.6$, rounded down to 30 shirts

8. $24.5 - 1.003 = 23.497$

9. $(\$265,830.25)(.0525) \approx \$13,956.09$

10. $\$67,507.50 \div \$22.50 \approx 3000$ transactions

11. $\$275,825,000 \div .945 \approx \$291,878,000$

12. $\$50,000,000 + \$1,500,000 - \$10,000,000 - \$37,500,000 = \$4,000,000$ Then, $\$4,000,000 \div \$50,000,000 = .08 = 8\%$

13. An increase of 300% over x = 4x, so sales are 4 times as large.

14. Gross sales $= \$374,000 \div .85 = \$440,000$

15. $(1.05)(1.03) = 1.0815$, which represents an 8.15% increase in dollar sales volume

16. $\$525 - \$310 = \$215$; then, $\frac{\$215}{\$525} \approx 40.9\%$

17. \$30 will represent 55% of retail amount. Thus, retail will be $\$30 \div .55 \approx \$54.50$

18. $(\$40)(.60) - \$1 = \$23$

19. $(\$17,000)(1.34) = \$22,780$. Then, $\$22,780 - \$6000 = \$16,780$. Also, $\$17,000 - \$3,000 = \$14,000$. Finally, $(\$16,780 - \$14,000) \div \$14,000 \approx 19.9\%$

20. Let x = markup percent. Then, $\frac{x-40}{x}$ = .13
    Solving, x ≈ 46

21. Cost = ($35)(.60) = $21

22. Let x = retail price. Then, $1.20 = .60x. Solving, x = $2.00

23. $50 = 25% of retail, so retail = $200. Thus, cost = $200 - $50
    = $150

24. Let x = overtime hours. Then, ($9.60)(40) + $14.40x = $470.40
    Solving, x = 6. Total hours worked = 46

25. 5x - 3x = $12,000. So, x = $6000. Clarke's share = (3)($6000)
    = $18,000

TEST 2

DIRECTIONS: Each question or incomplete statement is followed by several suggested answers or completions. Select the one that BEST answers the question or completes the statement. *PRINT THE LETTER OF THE CORRECT ANSWER IN THE SPACE AT THE RIGHT.*

1. Assume that you require 77 dozen felt practice golf balls.   1.___
   Which of the following represents the LOWEST bid for these balls?
   A. 41¢ per half-dozen less a 3% discount
   B. 83¢ per dozen less a 7½% discount
   C. 85¢ per dozen less a 10% discount
   D. $65.00 less a series discount of 3%, 2%

2. Assume that you require 1,944 rulers, packed 12 to the   2.___
   box, 18 boxes to the carton.
   Which of the following represents the LOWEST bid for these rulers?
   A. 5½¢ per ruler
   B. 6¢ for the first 750 rulers; 5½¢ for the next 750 rulers; 4½¢ for every ruler thereafter
   C. $11.85 per carton
   D. $110 less series discounts of 2%, 1%

3. Assume that you require 20 cartons of colored raffia, cel-   3.___
   lophane wrapped in one lb. packages, 50 packages to the carton.
   Which of the following represents the LOWEST bid for the raffia?
   A. 8¢ per lb.; 15¢ per carton packing charge; 20¢ per carton delivery charge
   B. 9¢ per lb. less a 3% discount
   C. 10¢ per lb. for the first 150 lbs.; 9¢ per lb. for the next 200 lbs.; 8¢ for each lb. thereafter
   D. $83.50 less a 4½% discount

4. Assume that you require 50 yards of table felt, 48" wide,   4.___
   and 12 yards of table felt, 72" wide.
   Which of the following represents the LOWEST bid for this felt?
   A. 32¢ per yard (48" wide), 40¢ per yard (72" wide)
   B. 34¢ per yard (48" wide), 43¢ per yard (72" wide); series discounts of 5%, 3%
   C. 36¢ per yard (48" wide), 41¢ per yard (72" wide); 8% discount, packing charge 75¢
   D. $23.00 for the order, 9% discount, packing charge 50¢

5. If the cost of 3 erasers is 5¢, the cost of 2½ dozen   5.___
   erasers is
      A. 18¢   B. 37½¢   C. 50¢   D. 31½¢

6. A circle graph of a budget shows the expenditure of 26.2%   6.___
   for housing, 28.4% for food, 12% for clothing, 12.7% for
   taxes, and the balance for miscellaneous items.
   The percent for miscellaneous items is
      A. 31.5   B. 79.3   C. 20.7   D. 68.5

7. The cost of a broadloom rug measuring 4 feet by 6 feet,   7.___
   at $6.30 per square yard, is
      A. $16.80   B. $50.40   C. $37.60   D. $21.00

8. The number of tiles each measuring 2 inches by 3 inches   8.___
   needed for a wall 3 feet high and 5 feet long is
      A. 180   B. 30   C. 360   D. 60

9. Assume that you require 4 tons of fertilizer. The ferti-   9.___
   lizer is packed in 100 pound bags.
   Which of the following represents the LOWEST bid for the
   fertilizer?
      A. 6¢ per pound
      B. $5.50 per bag
      C. $7.00 for each of the first 30 bags; $5.00 for each
         bag thereafter
      D. $500.00 less 3½% discount

10. Assume pencils are packed 5 gross to the case. A buyer   10.___
    requires 3,800 pencils each for three departments and
    2,700 pencils for another department. Assume that the
    vendor will ship unbroken cases only directly to each
    department.
    How many cases should he buy?
       A. 21   B. 22   C. 48   D. 49

11. Assume that a buyer had to purchase 40,000 lbs. of salt.   11.___
    Which one of the following bids should he accept,
    assuming quality, service, and delivery terms are all
    the same?
       A. 1¢ per pound, 2%-30 days
       B. 99¢ per 100 lbs., 1%-30 days
       C. $19 per ton, 1%-30 days
       D. $18 per ton, net-30 days

12. Which one of the following four bids represents the BEST   12.___
    value, assuming delivery costs amount to $100?
       A. $1,000 f.o.b. buyer, less 2%-10 days
       B. $900 f.o.b. seller, less 2%-10 days
       C. $975 delivered, net cash 30 days
       D. $990 f.o.b. buyer, less 1%-10 days

13. Suppose that four suppliers make the following offers to   13.___
    sell 2,000 units of a particular commodity.
    Which one is the MOST advantageous proposal?
       A. $10 list, less 40% and 5%
       B. $5 cost, plus 20% to cover overhead and profit
       C. $10 list, less 20% and 20%
       D. $5 cost, plus 10% overhead and 10% for profit

14. Suppose that you purchase 100 units of an item at a list   14.___
    of $1 per unit less 40% and 10%, and less 2% if paid
    within 10 days.
    If payment is made within the 10-day limit, the amount
    of the payment should be
       A. $52.92   B. $54.00   C. $58.80   D. $60.00

15. Assume that the 1987 cost of living factor was 100 and   15.___
    that a certain product was selling that year for $5 per
    unit. Assume further that at the present time the cost
    of living factor is 150.
    If the selling price of the product increased 10% more
    than the cost of living during this period, at the present
    time the product would be selling for _____ per unit.
       A. $8.25   B. $10.50   C. $16.50   D. $7.75

16. A certain food is sold in 4 ounce cans at 10 for $1.00   16.___
    and in 1 pound cans at 3 for $1.00.
    The savings in price per ounce by purchasing the food
    in the larger can is _____ cents/ounce.
       A. .53   B. .35   C. .42   D. .68

17. After an article is discounted at 25%, it sells for $375.   17.___
    The ORIGINAL price of the article was
       A. $93.75   B. $350   C. $375   D. $500

18. Assume that you require 1,440 pencils, packed 12 to the   18.___
    box, 24 boxes to the carton.
    Which of the following represents the LOWEST bid for
    these pencils?
       A. 2¢ per pencil
       B. $6.50 per carton
       C. 27¢ per box less a 4% discount
       D. $40 less a 3% discount

19. If erasers cost 8¢ each for the first 250, 7¢ each for   19.___
    the next 250, and 5¢ for every eraser thereafter, how
    many erasers may be purchased for $50?
       A. 600   B. 750   C. 850   D. 1,000

20. Assume that a buyer saves $14 on the purchase of an item   20.___
    that is discounted at 25%.
    The amount of money that the buyer must pay for the item
    is
       A. $42   B. $52   C. $54   D. $56

Questions 21-24.

DIRECTIONS: Questions 21 through 24 are to be answered on the basis
             of the following method of obtaining a reorder point:
             multiply the monthly rate of consumption by the lead
             time (in months) and add the minimum balance.

21. If the lead time is one-half month, the minimum balance
    is 6 units, and the monthly rate of consumption is 4
    units, then the reorder point is ____ units.   21.___
      A. 4   B. 6   C. 8   D. 12

22. If the reorder point is 25 units, the lead time is 3   22.___
    months, and the minimum balance is 10 units, then the
    average monthly rate of consumption is ____ units.
      A. 3   B. 5   C. 6   D. 10

23. If the reorder point is 400 units, the lead time is 2   23.___
    months, and the monthly rate of consumption is 150 units,
    then the minimum balance is ____ units.
      A. 50   B. 100   C. 150   D. 200

24. If the reorder point is 75 units, the monthly rate of   24.___
    consumption is 60 units, and the minimum balance is
    45 units, then the lead time is ____ month(s).
      A. $\frac{1}{2}$ B. 1   C. 2   D. 4

25. A purchasing office has 4,992 special requisitions to be   25.___
    processed. Working alone, Buyer A could process these in
    30 days; working alone, Buyer B could process these in 40
    days; working alone, Buyer C could process these in 60
    days.
    The LEAST number of days in which Buyers A, B, and C
    working together can process these 4,992 special requisi-
    tions is APPROXIMATELY ____ days.
      A. 14   B. 20   C. 34   D. 45

KEY (CORRECT ANSWERS)

1. C		11. D	
2. B		12. C	
3. D		13. A	
4. B		14. A	
5. C		15. A	
6. C		16. C	
7. A		17. D	
8. C		18. A	
9. B		19. B	
10. B		20. A	

21. C
22. B
23. B
24. A
25. A

SOLUTIONS TO PROBLEMS

1. Bid A = (.82)(77)(.97) ≈ $61.25; Bid B = (.83)(77)(.925) ≈ $59.12
Bid C = (.85)(77)(.90) ≈ $58.91; Bid D = ($65.00)(.97)(.98) ≈ $61
Thus, Bid C is lowest.

2. Bid A = (.055)(1944) = $106.92; Bid B = (.06)(750)+(.055)(750) +
(.045)(444) = $106.23; Bid C = ($11.85)(9) = $106.65;
Bid D = ($110)(.98)(.99) ≈ $106.72. Thus, Bid B is lowest.

3. Bid A = (.08)(1000)+(.15)(20)+(.20)(20) = $87.00
Bid B = (.09)(1000)(.97) = $87.30
Bid C = (.10)(150)+(.09)(200)+(.08)(650) = $85.00
Bid D = ($83.50)(.955) ≈ $79.74
Thus, Bid D is lowest.

4. Bid A = (.32)(50)+(.40)(12) = $20.80
Bid B = (.34)(50)+(.43)(12) = $22.16; so ($22.16)(.95)(.97) ≈ $20.
Bid C = (.36)(50)+(.41)(12) = $22.92; so ($22.92)(.92)+.75 ≈ $21.8
Bid D = ($23.00)(.91)+.50 = $21.43
Bid B is lowest.

5. $(2\frac{1}{2})(12)$ = 30 erasers, which will cost (.05)(10) = 50¢

6. 100 - 26.2 - 28.4 - 12 - 12.7 = 20.7% for miscellaneous items

7. $24 \div 9 = 2\frac{2}{3}$ sq.yds. Then, $(\$6.30)(2\frac{2}{3})$ = $16.80

8. 3' ÷ 2" = 18; 5' ÷ 3" = 20. Thus, (18)(20) = 360 tiles

9. Bid A = (.06)(8000) = $480
Bid B = ($5.50)(80) = $440
Bid C = ($7.00)(30)+($5.00)(50) = $460
Bid D = ($500)(.965) = $482.50
Thus, Bid B is lowest.

10. 5 gross = 5(144) = 720; 3800 will be 6 unbroken cases × 3 = 18
2700 will be 4 unbroken cases = 4
————
22

11. Bid A = (.01)(40,000)(.98) = $392.00
Bid B = (.99)(400)(.99) = $392.04
Bid C = ($19)(20)(.99) = $376.20
Bid D = ($18)(20) = $360.00
Bid D is lowest.

12. A. 1,000 - 2% = 980
B. 900 + 100 - 2% = 980
C. 975
D. 990 - 9.90 = 980.10

C is best value

13. Proposal A: ($10)(.60)(.95) = $5.70
     Proposal B: $5 + ($5)(.20) = $6.00
     Proposal C: ($10)(.80)(.80) = $6.40
     Proposal D: $5 + (.20)($5) = $6.00
     Proposal A is lowest.

14. Payment = ($100)(.60)(.90)(.98) = $52.92

15. Present cost = ($5)(1.50)(1.10) = $8.25

16. 40 ounces for $1.00 in smaller cans means 2.5 cents per ounce.
     For the larger cans, (3)(16) = 48 ounces for $1.00, which means
     2.08$\overline{3}$ cents per ounce. The savings is approximately .42 cents
     per ounce.

17. Original price = $375 ÷ .75 = $500

18. Bid A = (1440)(.02) = $28.80
     Bid B = (1440÷288)($6.50) = $32.50
     Bid C = [(1440÷12)(.27)][.96] ≈ $31.10
     Bid D = ($40)(.97) = $38.80
     Bid A is lowest.

19. 250 erasers cost (250)(.08) = $20
     500 erasers cost $20 + (250)(.07) = $37.50
     The number of additional erasers = ($50-$37.50) ÷ .05 = 250
     Total number of erasers = 750

20. $14 ÷ .25 = $56. Then, $56 - $14 = $42

21. (4)(.5) + 6 = 8 units

22. Let x = monthly rate. Then, (x)(3) + 10 = 25. Solving, x = 5 units

23. Let x = minimum balance. (150)(2) + x = 400. Solving, x = 100 units

24. Let x = lead time. (60)(x) + 45 = 75. Solving, x = ½ month

25. Buyer A does 4992 ÷ 30 ≈ 166 per day
     Buyer B does 4992 ÷ 40 ≈ 125 per day
     Buyer C does 4992 ÷ 60 ≈ 83 per day
     Working together, approximately 374 requisitions are done per day.
     Finally, 4992 ÷ 374 ≈ 13, closest to 14 in selections.

CLERICAL ABILITIES TEST
EXAMINATION SECTION

DIRECTIONS FOR THIS SECTION:
Each question or incomplete statement is followed by several suggested answers or completions. Select the one that *BEST* answers the question or completes the statement. *PRINT THE LETTER OF THE CORRECT ANSWER IN THE SPACE AT THE RIGHT.*

TEST 1

Questions 1 10.
DIRECTIONS: Questions 1 through 10 consist of lines of names, dates and numbers. For each question, you are to choose the option (A, B, C, or D) in Column II which *EXACTLY* matches the information in Column I. *PRINT THE LETTER OF THE CORRECT ANSWER IN THE SPACE AT THE RIGHT.*

SAMPLE QUESTION

Column I			Column II			
Schneider	11/16/75	581932	A. Schneider	11/16/75	518932	
			B. Schneider	11/16/75	581932	
			C. Schnieder	11/16/75	581932	
			D. Shnieder	11/16/75	518932	

The correct answer is B. Only option B shows the name, date and number exactly as they are in Column I. Option A has a mistake in the number. Option C has a mistake in the name. Option D has a mistake in the name and in the number.
Now answer Questions 1 through 10 in the same manner.

Column I				Column II			
1. Johnston	12/26/74	659251	A.	Johnson	12/23/74	659251	1. ...
			B.	Johston	12/26/74	659251	
			C.	Johnston	12/26/74	695251	
			D.	Johnston	12/26/74	659251	
2. Allison	1/26/75	9939256	A.	Allison	1/26/75	9939256	2. ...
			B.	Alisson	1/26/75	9939256	
			C.	Allison	1/26/76	9399256	
			D.	Allison	1/26/75	9993256	
3. Farrell	2/12/75	361251	A.	Farell	2/21/75	361251	3. ...
			B.	Farrell	2/12/75	361251	
			C.	Farrell	2/21/75	361251	
			D.	Farrell	2/12/75	361151	
4. Guerrero	4/28/72	105689	A.	Guererro	4/28/72	105689	4. ...
			B.	Guererro	4/28/72	105986	
			C.	Guerrero	4/28/72	105869	
			D.	Guerrero	4/28/72	105689	
5. McDonnell	6/05/73	478215	A.	McDonnell	6/15/73	478215	5. ...
			B.	McDonnell	6/05/73	478215	
			C.	McDonnell	6/05/73	472815	
			D.	MacDonell	6/05/73	478215	
6. Shepard	3/31/71	075421	A.	Sheperd	3/31/71	075421	6. ...
			B.	Shepard	3/13/71	075421	
			C.	Shepard	3/31/71	075421	
			D.	Shepard	3/13/71	075241	
7. Russell	4/01/69	031429	A.	Russell	4/01/69	031429	7. ...
			B.	Russell	4/10/69	034129	
			C.	Russell	4/10/69	031429	
			D.	Russell	4/01/69	034129	

8. Phillips   10/16/68   961042   A. Philipps   10/16/68 961042   8.
                                 B. Phillips   10/16/68 960142
                                 C. Phillips   10/16/68 961042
                                 D. Philipps   10/16/68 916042

9. Campbell   11/21/72   624856   A. Campbell   11/21/72 624856   9.
                                 B. Campbell   11/21/72 624586
                                 C. Campbell   11/21/72 624686
                                 D. Campbel   11/21/72 624856

10. Patterson 9/18/71 76199176   A. Patterson 9/18/72 76191976 10.
                                B. Patterson 9/18/71 76199176
                                C. Patterson 9/18/72 76199176
                                D. Patterson 9/18/71 76919176

Questions 11-15.
DIRECTIONS: Questions 11 through 15 consist of groups of numbers and letters which you are to compare. For each question, you are to choose the option (A, B, C, or D) in Column II which *EXACTLY* matches the group of numbers and letters given in Column I.

SAMPLE QUESTION

Column I
B92466

Column II
A. B92644
B. B94266
C. A92466
D. B92466

The correct answer is D. Only option D in Column II shows the group of numbers and letters *EXACTLY* as it appears in Column I.
Now answer Questions 11 through 15 in the same manner.

Column I

11.   925AC5

Column II
A. 952CA5   11.
B. 925AC5
C. 952AC5
D. 925CA6

12.   Y006925
A. Y060925   12.
B. Y006295
C. Y006529
D. Y006925

13.   J236956
A. J236956   13.
B. J326965
C. J239656
D. J932656

14.   AB6952
A. AB6952   14.
B. AB9625
C. AB9652
D. AB6925

15.   X259361
A. X529361   15.
B. X259631
C. X523961
D. X259361

Questions 16-25.
DIRECTIONS: Each of Questions 16 through 25 consists of three lines of code letters and three lines of numbers. The numbers on each line should correspond with the code letters on the same line in accordanc with the table below.

Code Letter	S	V	W	A	Q	M	X	E	G	K
Corresponding Number	0	1	2	3	4	5	6	7	8	9

On some of the lines, an error exists in the coding. Compare the letters and numbers in each question carefully. If you find an error or errors on:

    only *one* of the lines in the question, mark your answer A;

    any *two* lines in the question, mark your answer B;

    all *three* lines in the question, mark your answer C;

    none of the lines in the question, mark your answer D.

SAMPLE QUESTION

    WQGKSXG   2489068

    XEKVQMA   6591453

    KMAESXV   9527061

In the above example, the first line is correct since each code letter listed has the correct corresponding number. On the second line, an error exists because code letter E should have the number 7 instead of the number 5. On the third line an error exists because the code letter A should have the number 3 instead of the number 2. Since there are errors in two of the three lines, the correct answer is B. Now answer Questions 16 through 25 in the same manner.

16.	SWQEKGA	0247983	16. ...
	KEAVSXM	9731065	
	SSAXGKQ	0036894	
17.	QAMKMVS	4259510	17. ...
	MGGEASX	5897306	
	KSWMKWS	9125920	
18.	WKXQWVE	2964217	18. ...
	QKXXQVA	4966413	
	AWMXGVS	3253810	
19.	GMMKASE	8559307	19. ...
	AWVSKSW	3210902	
	QAVSVGK	4310189	
20.	XGKQSMK	6894049	20. ...
	QSVKEAS	4019730	
	GSMXKMV	8057951	
21.	AEKMWSG	3195208	21. ...
	MKQSVQK	5940149	
	XGQAEVW	6843712	
22.	XGMKAVS	6858310	22. ...
	SKMAWEQ	0953174	
	GVMEQSA	8167403	
23.	VQSKAVE	1489317	23. ...
	WQGKAEM	2489375	
	MEGKAWQ	5689324	
24.	XMQVSKG	6541098	24. ...
	QMEKEWS	4579720	
	KMEVKGA	9571983	
25.	GKVAMEW	8912572	25. ...
	AXMVKAE	3651937	
	KWAGMAV	9238531	

Questions 26-35.
DIRECTIONS: Each of Questions 26 through 35 consists of a column of figures. For each question, add the column of figures and choose the correct answer from the four choices given.

26. 5,665.43
    2,356.69
    6,447.24   A. 20,698.01   B. 21,709.01
    7,239.65   C. 21,718.01   D. 22,609.01   26. ..

27. 817,209.55
    264,354.29
    82,368.76   A. 1,893,997.49   B. 1,989,988.39
    849,964.89   C. 2,009,077.39   D. 2,013,897.49   27. ..

28. 156,366.89
    249,973.23
    823,229.49   A. 1,286,439.06   B. 1,287,521.06
    56,869.45   C. 1,297,539.06   D. 1,296,421.06   28. ..

29. 23,422.15
    149,696.24
    238,377.53
    86,289.79   A.   989,229.34   B.   999,879.34
    505 544.63   C. 1,003,330.34   D. 1,023,329.34   29. ..

30. 2,468,926.70
    656,842.28
    49,723.15   A. 3,218,061.72   B. 3,808,092.72
    832,369.59   C. 4,007,861.72   D. 4,818,192.72   30. ..

31. 524,201.52
    7,775,678.51
    8,345,299.63
    40,628,898.08 A. 88,646,647.81 B. 88,646,747.91
    31,374,670.07 C. 88,648,647.91 D. 88,648,747.81   31. ..

32. 6,824,829.40
    682,482.94
    5,542,015.27
    775,678.51   A. 21,557,513.37 B. 21,567,513.37
    7,732,507.25   C. 22,567,503.37 D. 22,567,513.37   32. ..

33. 22,109,405.58
    6 097 093.43
    5 050,073.99
    8,118,050.05   A. 45,688,593.87 B. 45,688,603.87
    4,313,980.82   C. 45,689,593.87 D. 45,689,603.87   33. ..

34. 79,324,114.19
    99,848,129.74
    43,331,653.31 A. 264,114,104.38   B. 264,114,114.38
    41,610,207.14 C. 265,114,114.38   D. 265,214,104.38   34. ..

35. 33,729,653.94
    5,959,342.58
    26,052,715,47
    4,452,669.52   A. 76,374,334.10   B. 76,375,334.10
    7,079,953.59   C. 77,274,335.10   D. 77,275,335.10   35. ..

4

Questions 36-40.
DIRECTIONS: Each of Questions 36 through 40 consists of a single
number in Column I and four options in Column II. For each question,
you are to choose the option (A, B, C, or D) in Column II which
EXACTLY matches the number in Column I.

SAMPLE QUESTION

Column I		Column II
5965121	A.	5956121
	B.	5965121
	C.	5966121
	D.	5965211

The correct answer is B. Only option B shows the number *EXACTLY* as
it appears in Column I.
Now answer Questions 36 through 40 in the same manner.

	Column I		Column II	
36.	9643242	A.	9643242	36. ...
		B.	9462342	
		C.	9642442	
		D.	9463242	
37.	3572477	A.	3752477	37. ...
		B.	3725477	
		C.	3572477	
		D.	3574277	
38.	5276101	A.	5267101	38. ...
		B.	5726011	
		C.	5271601	
		D.	5276101	
39.	4469329	A.	4496329	39. ...
		B.	4469329	
		C.	4496239	
		D.	4469239	
40.	2326308	A.	2236308	40. ...
		B.	2233608	
		C.	2326308	
		D.	2323608	

TEST 2

Questions 1-5.
DIRECTIONS: Each of Questions 1 through 5 consists of a name and
a dollar amount. In each question, the name and dollar amount in
Column II should be an exact copy of the name and dollar amount in
Column I. If there is:
   a mistake only in the name, mark your answer A;
   a mistake only in the dollar amount, mark your answer B;
   a mistake in both the name and the dollar amount, mark your answer C;
   no mistake in either the name or the dollar amount, mark your
   answer D.

SAMPLE QUESTION

Column I	Column II
George Peterson	George Petersson
$125.50	$125.50

5

Compare the name and dollar amount in Column II with the name and dollar amount in Column I. The name *Petersson* in Column II is spelle‹ *Peterson* in Column I. The amount is the same in both columns. Sinc‹ there is a mistake only in the name, the answer to the sample question is A.

Now answer Questions 1 through 5 in the same manner.

	Column I	Column II	
1.	Susanne Shultz $3440	Susanne Schultz $3440	1. .
2.	Anibal P. Contrucci $2121.61	Anibel P. Contrucci $2112.61	2. .
3.	Eugenio Mendoza $12.45	Eugenio Mendozza $12.45	3. .
4.	Maurice Gluckstadt $4297	Maurice Gluckstadt $4297	4. .
5.	John Pampellonne $4656.94	John Pammpellonne $4566.94	5. .

Questions 6-11.

DIRECTIONS: Each of Questions 6 through 11 consists of a set of names and addresses which you are to compare. In each question, th‹ name and addresses in Column II should be an *EXACT* copy of the name and address in Column I. If there is:

    a mistake only in the name, mark your answer A;
    a mistake only in the address, mark your answer B;
    a mistake in both the name and address, mark your answer C;
    no mistake in either the name or address, mark your answer D.

SAMPLE QUESTION

Column I	Column II
Michael Filbert	Michael Filbert
456 Reade Street	645 Reade Street
New York, N. Y. 10013	New York, N. Y. 10013

Since there is a mistake only in the address (the street number should be 456 instead of 645), the answer to the sample question is B.

Now answer Questions 6 through 11 in the same manner.

	Column I	Column II	
6.	Hilda Goettelmann 55 Lenox Rd. Brooklyn, N. Y. 11226	Hilda Goetteleman 55 Lenox Ave. Brooklyn, N. Y. 11226	6. .
7.	Arthur Sherman 2522 Batchelder St. Brooklyn, N. Y. 11235	Arthur Sharman 2522 Batcheder St. Brooklyn, N. Y. 11253	7. .
8.	Ralph Barnett 300 West 28 Street New York, New York 10001	Ralph Barnett 300 West 28 Street New York, New York 10001	8. .
9.	George Goodwin 135 Palmer Avenue Staten Island, New York 10302	George Godwin 135 Palmer Avenue Staten Island, New York 10302	9. .
10.	Alonso Ramirez 232 West 79 Street New York, N. Y. 10024	Alonso Ramirez 223 West 79 Street New York, N. Y. 10024	10. .
11.	Cynthia Graham 149-35 83 Street Howard Beach, N. Y. 11414	Cynthia Graham 149-35 83 Street Howard Beach, N. Y. 11414	11. .

Questions 12-20.
DIRECTIONS: Questions 12 through 20 are problems in subtraction. For each question do the subtraction and select your answer from the four choices given.

12. 232,921.85   A. 52,433.17 B. 52,434.17   12. ...
    -179,587.68   C. 53,334.17 D. 53,343.17

13. 5,531,876.29   A. 1,634,717.93 B. 1,644,718.93   13. ...
    -3,897,158.36   C. 1,734,717.93 D. 1,734,718.93

14. 1,482,658.22   A. 544,633.46 B. 544,732.46   14. ...
    - 937,925.76   C. 545,632.46 D. 545,732.46

15. 937,828.17   A. 678,154.29 B. 679,154.29   15. ...
    -259,673.88   C. 688,155.39 D. 699,155.39

16. 760,412.38   A. 496,046.43 B. 496,946.43   16. ...
    -263,465.95   C. 496,956.43 D. 497,046.43

17. 3,203,902.26   A. 260,814.30 B. 269,824.30   17. ...
    -2,933,087.96   C. 270,814.30 D. 270,824.30

18. 1,023,468.71   A. 88,780.83 B. 88,789.83   18. ...
    - 934,678.88   C. 88,880.83 D. 88,889.83

19. 831,549.47   A. 58,734.69 B. 58,834.69   19. ...
    -772,814.78   C. 59,735.69 D. 59,834.69

20. 6,306,281.74   A. 2,687,904.99 B. 2,688,904.99   20. ...
    -3,617,376.75   C. 2,689,804.99 D. 2,799,905.99

Questions 21-30.
DIRECTIONS: Each of Questions 21 through 30 consists of three lines of code letters and three lines of numbers. The numbers on each line should correspond with the code letters on the same line in accordance with the table below.

Code Letter	J	U	B	T	Y	D	K	R	L	P
Corresponding Number	0	1	2	3	4	5	6	7	8	9

On some of the lines, an error exists in the coding. Compare the letters and numbers in each question carefully. If you find an error or errors on:
    only *one* of the lines in the question, mark your answer A;
    any *two* lines in the question, mark your answer B;
    all *three* lines in the question, mark your answer C;
    none of the lines in the question, mark your answer D.

SAMPLE QUESTION

    BJRPYUR   2079417
    DTBPYKJ   5328460
    YKLDBLT   4685283

In the above sample the first line is correct since each code letter listed has the correct corresponding number. On the second line, an error exists because code letter P should have the number 9 instead of the number 8. The third line is correct since each code letter listed has the correct corresponding number. Since there is an error in *one* of the three lines, the correct answer is A.
Now answer Questions 21 through 30 in the same manner.

7

21.	BYPDTJL	2495308	21.
	PLRDTJU	9815301	
	DTJRYLK	5207486	
22.	RPBYRJK	7934706	22.
	PKTYLBU	9624821	
	KDLPJYR	6489047	
23.	TPYBUJR	3942107	23.
	BYRKPTU	2476931	
	DUKPYDL	5169458	
24.	KBYDLPL	6345898	24.
	BLRKBRU	2876261	
	JTULDYB	0318542	
25.	LDPYDKR	8594567	25.
	BDKDRJL	2565708	
	BDRPLUJ	2679810	
26.	PLRLBPU	9858291	26.
	LPYKRDJ	8936750	
	TDKPDTR	3569527	
27.	RKURPBY	7617924	27.
	RYUKPTJ	7426930	
	RTKPTJD	7369305	
28.	DYKPBJT	5469203	28.
	KLPJBTL	6890238	
	TKPLBJP	3698209	
29.	BTPRJYL	2397148	29.
	LDKUTYR	8561347	
	YDBLRPJ	4528190	
30.	ULPBKYT	1892643	30.
	KPDTRBJ	6953720	
	YLKJPTB	4860932	

KEYS (CORRECT ANSWERS)

TEST 1

1. D	11. B	21. A	31. D
2. A	12. D	22. C	32. A
3. B	13. A	23. B	33. B
4. D	14. A	24. D	34. A
5. B	15. D	25. A	35. C
6. C	16. D	26. B	36. A
7. A	17. C	27. D	37. C
8. C	18. A	28. A	38. D
9. A	19. D	29. C	39. B
10. B	20. B	30. C	40. C

TEST 2

1. A	11. D	21. B
2. C	12. C	22. C
3. A	13. A	23. D
4. D	14. B	24. B
5. C	15. A	25. A
6. C	16. B	26. C
7. C	17. C	27. A
8. D	18. B	28. D
9. A	19. A	29. B
10. B	20. B	30. D

NAME and NUMBER COMPARISON

COMMENTARY

This test seeks to measure your ability and disposition to do a job carefully and accurately, your attention to exactness and preciseness of detail, your alertness and versatility in discerning similarities and differences between things, and your power in systematically handling written language symbols.

It is actually a test of your ability to do academic and/or clerical work, using the basic elements of verbal (qualitative) and mathematical (quantitative) learning - words and numbers.

EXAMINATION SECTION
TEST 1

Questions 1-6.

DIRECTIONS: Questions 1 through 6 consist of sets of names and addresses. In each question, the name and address in Column II should be an exact copy of the name and address in Column I. *PRINT IN THE SPACE AT THE RIGHT THE LETTER*
   A. if there is a mistake only in the name
   B. if there is a mistake only in the address
   C. if there is a mistake in both name and address
   D. if there is no mistake in either name or address

SAMPLE QUESTION

Column I	Column II
Michael Filbert	Michael Filbert
456 Reade Street	645 Reade Street
New York, N.Y. 10013	New York, N.Y. 10013

Since there is a mistake only in the address (the street number should be 456 instead of 645), the answer to the sample question is B.

	Column I	Column II	
1.	Esta Wong	Esta Wang	1. ...
	141 West 68 St.	141 West 68 St.	
	New York, N.Y. 10023	New York, N.Y. 10023	
2.	Dr. Alberto Grosso	Dr. Alberto Grosso	2. ...
	3475 12th Avenue	3475 12th Avenue	
	Brooklyn, N.Y. 11218	Brooklyn, N.Y. 11218	
3.	Mrs. Ruth Bortlas	Ms. Ruth Bortlas	3. ...
	482 Theresa Ct.	482 Theresa Ct.	
	Far Rockaway, N.Y. 11691	Far Rockaway, N.Y. 11169	
4.	Mr. and Mrs. Howard Fox	Mr. and Mrs. Howard Fox	4. ...
	2301 Sedgwick Ave.	231 Sedgwick Ave.	
	Bronx, N.Y. 10468	Bronx, N.Y. 10468	
5.	Miss Marjorie Black	Miss Margorie Black	5. ...
	223 East 23 Street	223 East 23 Street	
	New York, N.Y. 10010	New York, N.Y. 10010	
6.	Michelle Herman	Michelle Hermann	6. ...
	806 Valley Rd.	806 Valley Dr.	
	Old Tappan, N.J. 07675	Old Tappan, N.J. 07675	

TEST 2

Questions 1-6.

DIRECTIONS: Questions 1 through 6 consist of sets of names and addresses. In each question, the name and address in Column II should be an exact copy of the name and address in Column I. *PRINT IN THE SPACE AT THE RIGHT THE LETTER*

    A. if there is a mistake only in the name
    B. if there is a mistake only in the address
    C. if there is a mistake in both name and address
    D. if there is no mistake in either name or address

SAMPLE QUESTION

Column I	Column II
Christina Magnusson	Christina Magnusson
288 Greene Street	288 Greene Street
New York, N.Y. 10003	New York, N.Y. 10013

Since there is a mistake only in the address (the zone number should be 10003 instead of 10013), the answer to the sample question is B.

Column I	Column II	
1. Ms. Joan Kelly 313 Franklin Ave. Brooklyn, N.Y. 11202	Ms. Joan Kielly 318 Franklin Ave. Brooklyn, N.Y. 11202	1. ...
2. Mrs. Eileen Engel 47-24 86 Road Queens, N.Y. 11122	Mrs. Ellen Engel 47-24 86 Road Queens, N.Y. 11122	2. ...
3. Marcia Michaels 213 E. 81 St. New York, N.Y. 10012	Marcia Michaels 213 E. 81 St. New York, N.Y. 10012	3. ...
4. Rev. Edward J. Smyth 1401 Brandeis Street San Francisco, Calif. 96201	Rev. Edward J. Smyth 1401 Brandies Street San Francisco, Calif. 96201	4. ...
5. Alicia Rodriguez 24-68 81 St. Elmhurst, N.Y. 11122	Alicia Rodriquez 2468 81 St. Elmhurst, N.Y. 11122	5. ...
6. Ernest Eisemann 21 Columbia St. New York, N.Y. 10007	Ernest Eisermann 21 Columbia St. New York, N.Y. 10007	6. ...

TEST 3

Questions 1-8.
DIRECTIONS: Questions 1 through 8 consist of names, locations, and telephone numbers. In each question, the name, location, and telephone number in Column II should be an exact copy of the name, location, and telephone number in Column I. *PRINT IN THE SPACE AT THE RIGHT THE LETTER*

    A. if there is a mistake in *ONE* line only
    B. if there is a mistake in *TWO* lines only
    C. if there is a mistake in all *THREE* lines
    D. if there is *NO* mistake in any of the lines

Column I	Column II	
1. Ruth Lang EAM Bldg., Room C101 625-2000, ext. 765	Ruth Lang EAM Bldg., Room C110 625-2000, ext. 765	1. ...
2. Anne Marie Ionozzi Investigations, Room 827 576-4000, ext. 832	Anna Marie Ionozzi Investigation, Room 827 566-4000, ext. 832	2. ...

3. Willard Jameson   Willard Jamieson   3. ...
   Fm C Bldg., Room 687   Fm C Bldg., Room 687
   454-3010   454-3010

4. Joanne Zimmermann   Joanne Zimmermann   4. ...
   Bldg. SW, Room 314   Bldg. SW, Room 314
   532-4601   532-4601

5. Carlyle Whetstone   Caryle Whetstone   5. ...
   Payroll Division-A, Room212A Payroll Division-A, Room 212A
   262-5000, ext. 471   262-5000, ext. 417

6. Kenneth Chiang   Kenneth Chiang   6. ...
   Legal Council, Room 9745   Legal Counsel, Room 9745
   (201) 416-9100, ext. 17   (201) 416-9100, ext. 17

7. Ethel Koenig   Ethel Hoenig   7. ...
   Personnel Services Div,Rm433 Personal Services Div,Rm433
   635-7572   635-7527

8. Joyce Ehrhardt   Joyce Ehrhart   8. ...
   Office of the Administrator, Office of the Administrator,
                  Rm W56   Rm W56
   387-8706   387-7806

TEST 4

Questions 1-10.
DIRECTIONS: Each of Questions 1 through 10 gives the identification
number and name of a person who has received treatment at a certain
hospital. You are to choose the option (A, B, C, or D) which has
EXACTLY the same identification number and name as those given in
the question.

SAMPLE QUESTION

123765 Frank Y. Jones   A. 123675 Frank Y. Jones
                          B. 123765 Frank T. Jones
                          C. 123765 Frank Y. Johns
                          D. 123765 Frank Y. Jones

The correct answer is D. Only option D shows the identification
number and name exactly as they are in the sample question. Option A
has a mistake in the identification number. Option B has a mistake
in the middle initial of the name. Option C has a mistake in the
last name.
Now answer Questions 1 through 10 in the same manner.

1. 754898 Diane Malloy   A. 745898 Diane Malloy   1. ...
                            B. 754898 Dion Malloy
                            C. 754898 Diane Malloy
                            D. 754898 Diane Maloy

2. 661818 Ferdinand Figueroa A. 661818 Ferdinand Figeuroa 2. ...
                            B. 661618 Ferdinand Figueroa
                            C. 661818 Ferdnand Figueroa
                            D. 661818 Ferdinand Figueroa

3. 100101 Norman D. Braustein A. 100101 Norman D. Braustein 3. ...
                            B. 101001 Norman D. Braustein
                            C. 100101 Norman P. Braustien
                            D. 100101 Norman D. Bruastein

4. 838696 Robert Kittredge   A. 838969 Robert Kittredge   4. ...
                            B. 838696 Robert Kittredge
                            C. 388696 Robert Kittredge
                            D. 838696 Robert Kittridge

5. 243716 Abraham Soletsky

A. 243716 Abrahm Soletsky 5. ...
B. 243716 Abraham Solestky
C. 243176 Abraham Soletsky
D. 243716 Abraham Soletsky

6. 981121 Phillip M. Maas

A. 981121 Phillip M. Mass 6. ...
B. 981211 Phillip M. Maas
C. 981121 Phillip M. Maas
D. 981121 Phillip N. Maas

7. 786556 George Macalusso

A. 785656 George Macalusso 7. ...
B. 786556 George Macalusso
C. 786556 George Maculasso
D. 786556 George Macluasso

8. 639472 Eugene Weber

A. 639472 Eugene Weber 8. ...
B. 639472 Eugene Webre
C. 693472 Eugene Weber
D. 639742 Eugene Weber

9. 724936 John J. Lomonaco

A. 724936 John J. Lomanoco 9. ...
B. 724396 John L. Lomonaco
C. 724936 John J. Lomonaco
D. 724936 John J. Lamonaco

10. 899868 Michael Schnitzer

A. 899868 Micheal Schnitzer 10. ...
B. 898968 Michael Schnizter
C. 899688 Michael Schnitzer
D. 899868 Michael Schnitzer

KEYS (CORRECT ANSWERS)

TEST 1	TEST 2	TEST 3	TEST 4
1. A	1. C	1. A	1. C
2. D	2. A	2. C	2. D
3. C	3. D	3. A	3. A
4. B	4. B	4. D	4. B
5. A	5. C	5. B	5. D
6. C	6. A	6. A	6. C
		7. C	7. B
		8. B	8. A
			9. C
			10. D

4

NAME AND NUMBER CHECKING
EXAMINATION SECTION

DIRECTIONS FOR THIS SECTION: This test is designed to measure your speed and accuracy. You are urged to work both quickly and accurately and to do correctly as many lists as you can in the time allowed. The test consists of lists of pairs of names and numbers. Count the number of IDENTICAL pairs in each list. Then, select the correct number, 1, 2, 3, 4, or 5, and indicate your choice by circling the corresponding number on your answer paper.

Two sample questions are presented for your guidance, together with the correct solutions.

SAMPLE QUESTIONS

SAMPLE LIST A

CIRCLE
CORRECT ANSWER
1 2 3 4 5

    Adelphi College - Adelphia College
    Braxton Corp.   - Braxeton Corp.
    Wassaic State School- Wassaic State School
    Central Islip State Hospital- Central Isllip State
    Greenwich House - Greenwich House

NOTE that there are only two correct pairs - Wassaic State School and Greenwich House. Therefore, the CORRECT answer is 2.

SAMPLE LIST B
    78453694 - 78453684   1 2 3 4 5
    784530   - 784530
    533   - 534
    67845   - 67845
    2368745 - 2368755

NOTE that there are only two correct pairs - 784530 and 67845. Therefore, the CORRECT answer is 2.

TEST 1

LIST 1
    98654327   - 98654327   1 2 3 4 5
    74932564   - 74922564
    61438652   - 61438652
    01297653   - 01287653
    1865439765 - 1865439765

LIST 2
    478362   - 478363   1 2 3 4 5
    278354792 - 278354772
    9327   - 9327
    297384625 - 27384625
    6428156   - 6428158

LIST 3
    Abbey House   - Abbey House   1 2 3 4 5
    Actors' Fund Home   - Actor's Fund Home
    Adrian Memorial   - Adrian Memorial
    A. Clayton Powell Home - Clayton Powell House
    Abott E. Kittredge Club - Abbott E. Kitteredge Club

1

<u>LIST 4</u>
```
3682            - 3692
21937453829   - 31937453829
723            - 733
2763920        - 2763920
47293          - 47293
```
1   2   3   4   5

<u>LIST 5</u>
```
Adra House                  - Adra House
Adolescents' Court          - Adolescents' Court
Cliff Villa                 - Cliff Villa
Clark Neighborhood House    - Clark Neighborhood House
Alma Mathews House          - Alma Mathews House
```
1   2   3   4   5

<u>LIST 6</u>
```
28734291      - 28734271
63810263849   - 63810263846
26831027      - 26831027
368291        - 368291
7238102637    - 7238102637
```
1   2   3   4   5

<u>LIST 7</u>
```
Albion State T.S.        - Albion State T.C.
Clara de Hirsch Home     - Clara De Hirsch Home
Alice Carrington Royce   - Alice Carington Royce
Alice Chopin Nursery     - Alice Chapin Nursery
Lighthouse Eye Clinic    - Lighthouse Eye Clinic
```
1   2   3   4   5

<u>LIST 8</u>
```
327             - 329
712438291026   - 712438291026
2753829142     - 275382942
826287         - 826289
26435162839    - 26435162839
```
1   2   3   4   5

<u>LIST 9</u>
```
Letchworth Village   - Letchworth Village
A.A.A.E. Inc.        - A.A.A.E. Inc.
Clear Pool Camp      - Clear Pool Camp
A.M.M.L.A. Inc.      - A.M.M.L.A. Inc.
J.G. Harbard         - J.G. Harbord
```
1   2   3   4   5

<u>LIST 10</u>
```
8254           - 8256
2641526        - 2641526
4126389012     - 4126389102
725            - 725
76253917287    - 76253917287
```
1   2   3   4   5

<u>LIST 11</u>
```
Attica State Prison      - Attica State Prison
Nellie Murrah            - Nellie Murrah
Club Marshall            - Club Marshal
Assissium Casea-Maria    - Assissium Casa-Maria
The Homestead            - The Homestead
```
1   2   3   4   5

LIST 12
2691	- 2691	
623819253627	- 623819253629	
28637	- 28937	
278392736	- 278392736	
52739	- 52739	

1   2   3   4   5

LIST 13
A.I.C.P. Boys Camp	- A.I.C.P. Boy's Camp
Einar Chrystie	- Einar Christyie
Astoria Center	- Astoria Center
G. Frederick Brown	- G. Federick Browne
Vacation Service	- Vacation Services

1   2   3   4   5

LIST 14
728352689	- 728352688
643728	- 643728
37829176	- 37827196
8425367	- 8425369
65382018	- 65382018

1   2   3   4   5

LIST 15
E.S. Streim	- E.S. Strim
Charles E. Higgins	- Charles E. Higgins
Baluvelt, N.Y.	- Blauwelt, N.Y.
Roberta Magdalen	- Roberto Magdalen
Ballard School	- Ballard School

1   2   3   4   5

LIST 16
7382	- 7392
281374538299	- 291374538299
623	- 633
6273730	- 6273730
63392	- 63392

1   2   3   4   5

LIST 17
Orrin Otis	- Orrin Otis
Barat Settlement	- Barat Settlemen
Emmanuel House	- Emmanuel House
William T. McCreery	- William T. McCreery
Seamen's Home	- Seaman's Home

1   2   3   4   5

LIST 18
72824391	- 72834371
3729106237	- 37291106237
82620163849	- 82620163846
37638921	- 37638921
82631027	- 82631027

1   2   3   4   5

LIST 19
Commonwealth Fund	- Commonwealth Fund
Anne Johnsen	- Anne Johnson
Bide-a-Wee Home	- Bide-a-Wee Home
Riverdale-on-Hudson	- Riverdal-on-Hudson
Bialystoker Home	- Bailystoker Home

1   2   3   4   5

LIST 20
```
9271             - 9271
392918352627  - 392018852629
72637          - 72637
927392736      - 927392736
92739          - 92739
```
1 2 3 4 5

LIST 21
```
Charles M. Stump      - Charles M. Stump
Bourne Workshop       - Buorne Workshop
B'nai Bi'rith         - B'nai Brith
Poppenhuesen Institute - Poppenheusen Institute
Consular Service      - Consular Service
```
1 2 3 4 5

LIST 22
```
927352689   - 927352688
647382      - 648382
93729176    - 93727196
649536718   - 649536718
5835367     - 5835369
```
1 2 3 4 5

LIST 23
```
L.S. Bestend      - L.S. Bestent
Hirsch Mfg. Co.   - Hircsh Mfg. Co.
F.H. Storrs       - F.P. Storrs
Camp Wassaic      - Camp Wassaic
George Ballingham - George Ballingham
```
1 2 3 4 5

LIST 24
```
372846392048 - 372846392048
334          - 334
7283524678   - 7283524678
7283         - 7283
7283629372   - 7283629372
```
1 2 3 4 5

LIST 25
```
Dr. Stiles Company - Dr. Stills Company
Frances Hunsdon    - Frances Hunsdon
Northrop Barrert   - Nothrup Barrent
J. D. Brunjes      - J. D. Brunjes
Theo. Claudel & Co.- Theo. Claudel co.
```
1 2 3 4 5

TEST 2

LIST 1
```
82728        - 82738
82736292637  - 82736292639
728          - 738
83926192527  - 83726192529
82736272     - 82736272
```
1 2 3 4 5

LIST 2
    L. Pietri   - L. Pietri   1 2 3 4 5
    Mathewson, L.F.   - Mathewson, L.F.
    Funk & Wagnall   - Funk & Wagnalls
    Shimizu, Sojio   - Shimizu, Sojio
    Filing Equipment Bureau   - Filing Equipment Bureau

LIST 3
    63801829374   - 63801839474   1 2 3 4 5
    283577657   - 283577657
    65689   - 65689
    3457892026   - 3547893026
    2779   - 2778

LIST 4
    August Caille   - August Caille   1 2 3 4 5
    The Well-Fare Service   - The Wel-Fare Service
    K.L.M. Process Co.   - R.L.M. Process Co.
    Merrill Littell   - Merrill Littell
    Dodd & Sons   - Dodd & Son

LIST 5
    998745732   - 998745733   1 2 3 4 5
    723   - 723
    463849102983   - 463849102983
    8570   - 8570
    279012   - 279012

LIST 6
    M. A. Wender   - M.A. Winder   1 2 3 4 5
    Minneapolis Supply Co.   - Minneapolis Supply Co.
    Beverly Hills Corp.   - Beverley Hills Corp.
    Trafalgar Square   - Trafalgar Square
    Phifer, D.T.   - Phiefer, D.T.

LIST 7
    7834629   - 7834629   1 2 3 4 5
    3549806746   - 3549806746
    97802564   - 97892564
    689246   - 688246
    2578024683   - 2578024683

LIST 8
    Scadrons'   - Scadrons'   1 2 3 4 5
    Gensen & Bro.   - Genson & Bro.
    Firestone Co.   - Firestone Co.
    H.L. Eklund   - H.L. Eklund
    Oleomargarine Co.   - Oleomargarine Co.

LIST 9
    782039485618   - 782039485618   1 2 3 4 5
    53829172639   - 63829172639
    892   - 892
    829374820   - 829374820
    52937456   - 53937456

5

LIST 10
   First Nat'l Bank   - First Nat'l Bank   1 2 3 4 5
   Sedgwick Machine Works - Sedgewick Machine Works
   Hectographia Co.   - Hectographia Corp.
   Levet Bros.   - Levet Bros.
   Multistamp Co.,Inc. - Multistamp Co.,Inc.

LIST 11
   7293   - 7293   1 2 3 4 5
   6382910293   - 6382910292
   981928374012 - 981928374912
   58293   - 58393
   18203649271 - 283019283745

LIST 12
   Lowrey Lb'r Co.   - Lowrey Lb'r Co.   1 2 3 4 5
   Fidelity Service   - Fidelity Service
   Reumann, J.A.   - Reumann, J.A.
   Duophoto Ltd.   - Duophotos Ltd.
   John Jarratt   - John Jaratt

LIST 13
   6820384   - 6820384   1 2 3 4 5
   383019283745 - 383019283745
   63927102   - 63928102
   91029354829 - 91029354829
   58291728   - 58291728

LIST 14
   Standard Press Co. - Standard Press Co.   1 2 3 4 5
   Reliant Mf'g. Co.   - Relant Mf'g Co.
   M.C. Lynn   - M.C. Lynn
   J. Fredericks Company - G. Fredericks Company
   Wandermann, B.S.   - Wanderman, B.S.

LIST 15
   4283910293   - 4283010203   1 2 3 4 5
   992018273648 - 992018273848
   620   - 629
   752937273   - 752937373
   5392   - 5392

LIST 16
   Waldorf Hotel   - Waldorf Hotel   1 2 3 4 5
   Aaron Machinery Co. - Aaron Machinery Co.
   Caroline Ann Locke - Caroline Anne Locke
   McCabe Mfg. Co.   - McCabe Mfg. Co.
   R.L. Landres   - R.L. Landers

LIST 17
   68391028364 - 68391028394
   68293   - 68293   1 2 3 4 5
   739201   - 739201
   72839201   - 72839211
   739917   - 739719

LIST 18
   Balsam M.M.   - Balsamm, M.M.   1   2   3   4   5
   Steinway & Co.   - Stienway & M. Co.
   Eugene Elliott   - Eugene A. Elliott
   Leonard Loan Co.   - Leonard Loan Co.
   Frederick Morgan   - Frederick Morgen

LIST 19
   8929   - 9820   1   2   3   4   5
   392836472829   - 392836472829
   462   - 462
   2039271827   - 2039276837
   53829   - 54829

LIST 20
   Danielson's Hofbrau - Danielson's Hafbrau   1   2   3   4   5
   Edward A. Truarme   - Edward A. Truame
   Insulite Co.   - Insulite Co.
   Reisler Shoe Corp,   - Rielser Shoe Corp.
   L.L. Thompson   - L.L. Thompson

LIST 21
   92839102837   - 92839102837   1   2   3   4   5
   58891028   - 58891028
   7291728   - 7291928
   272839102839   - 272839102839
   428192   - 428102

LIST 22
   K.L. Veiller   - K.L. Veiller   1   2   3   4   5
   Webster, Roy   - Webster, Ray
   Drasner Spring Co.   - Drasner Spring Co.
   Edward J. Cravenport - Edward J. Cravanport
   Harold Field   - Harold A. Field

LIST 23
   2293   - 2293   1   2   3   4   5
   4283910293   - 5382910292
   871928374012   - 871928374912
   68293   - 68393
   81203649271   - 81293649271

LIST 24
   Tappe, Inc.   - Tappe, Inc.   1   2   3   4   5
   A.M. Wentingworth   - A.M. Wentinworth
   Scott A. Elliott   - Scott A. Elliott
   Echeverria Corp.   - Echeverria Corp.
   Bradford Victor Company - Bradford Victer Company

LIST 25
   4820384   - 4820384   1   2   3   4   5
   393019283745   - 283919283745
   63927102   - 63927102
   91029354829   - 91029354829
   48291728   - 48291728

KEYS (CORRECT ANSWERS)

TEST 1

1.	3
2.	1
3.	2
4.	2
5.	5

11.	3
12.	3
13.	1
14.	2
15.	2

6.	3
7.	1
8.	2
9.	4
10.	3

16.	2
17.	3
18.	2
19.	2
20.	4

21.	2
22.	1
23.	2
24.	5
25.	2

TEST 2

1.	1
2.	3
3.	2
4.	2
5.	4

11.	1
12.	3
13.	4
14.	2
15.	1

6.	2
7.	3
8.	4
9.	3
10.	3

16.	3
17.	2
18.	1
19.	2
20.	2

21.	3
22.	2
23.	1
24.	3
25.	4

CODING

EXAMINATION SECTION

COMMENTARY

An ingenious question-type called coding, involving elements of alphabetizing, filing, name and number comparison, and evaluative judgment and application, has currently won wide acceptance in testing circles for measuring clerical aptitude and general ability, particularly on the senior (middle) grades (levels).

While the directions for this question usually vary in detail, the candidate is generally asked to consider groups of names, codes, and numbers, and, then, according to a given plan, to arrange codes in alphabetic order; to arrange these in numerical sequence; to re-arrange columns of names and numbers in correct order; to espy errors in coding; to choose the correct coding arrangement in consonance with the given directions and examples, etc.

This question-type appears to have few parameters in respect to form, substance, or degree of difficulty.

Accordingly, acquaintance with, and practice in, the coding question is recommended for the serious candidate.

___

EXAMINATION SECTION

TEST 1

DIRECTIONS FOR THIS SECTION: Questions 1 through 10 are to be answered on the basis of the following Code Table. In this table every letter has a corresponding code number to be punched. Each question contains three lines of letters and code numbers. In each line, the code numbers should correspond with the letters in accordance with the table.

Letter	M	X	R	T	W	A	E	Q	Z	C
Code	1	2	3	4	5	6	7	8	9	0

On some of the lines, an error exists in the coding. Compare the letters and numbers in each question carefully. If you find an error or errors on

only *one* of the lines in the question, mark your answer A;
any *two* lines in the question, mark your answer B;
all *three* lines in the question, mark your answer C;
none of the lines in the question, mark your answer D.

SAMPLE QUESTION

XAQMZMRQ	–	26819138
RAERQEX	–	3573872
TMZCMTZA	–	46901496

In the above sample, the first line is correct since each letter, as listed, has the correct corresponding code number.

In the second line, an error exists because the letter A should have the code number 6 instead of 5.

In the third line, an error exists because the letter W should have the code number 5 instead of 6.

Since there are errors in two of the three lines, your answer should be B.

1.	EQRMATTR	–	78316443
	MACWXRQW	–	16052385
	XZEMCAR	–	2971063
2.	CZEMRXQ	–	0971238
	XMTARET	–	2146374
	WCEARWEC	–	50863570
3.	CEXAWRQZ	–	07265389
	RCRMMZQT	–	33011984
	ACMZWTEX	–	60195472
4.	XRCZQZWR	–	23089953
	CMRQCAET	–	01389574
	ZXRWTECM	–	92345701
5.	AXMTRAWR	–	62134653
	EQQCZCEW	–	77809075
	MAZQARTM	–	16086341
6.	WRWQCTRM	–	53580431
	CXMWAERZ	–	02156739
	RCQEWWME	–	30865517
7.	CRMECEAX	–	03170762
	MZCTRXRQ	–	19043238
	XXZREMEW	–	22937175
8.	MRCXQEAX	–	13928762
	WAMZTRMZ	–	65194319
	ECXARWXC	–	70263520
9.	MAWXECRQ	–	16527038
	RXQEAETM	–	32876741
	RXEWMCZQ	–	32751098
10.	MRQZCATE	–	13890647
	WCETRXAW	–	50743625
	CZWMCERT	–	09510734

1. ...

2. ...

3. ...

4. ...

5. ...

6. ...

7. ...

8. ...

9. ...

10. ...

TEST 2

DIRECTIONS FOR THIS SECTION: Questions 1 through 6 consist of three
lines of code letters and numbers. The numbers on each line should
correspond with the code letters on the same line in accordance with
the table below.

Code Letter	F	X	L	M	R	W	T	S	B	H
Corresponding Number	0	1	2	3	4	5	6	7	8	9

On some of the lines, an error exists in the coding. Compare the
letters and numbers in each question carefully. If you find an error
or errors on
    only *one* of the lines in the question, mark your answer A;
    any *two* lines in the question, mark your answer B;
    all *three* lines in the question, mark your answer C;
    none of the lines in the question, mark your answer D.

2

SAMPLE QUESTION

```
LTSXHMF 2671930
TBRWHLM 6845913
SXLBFMR 5128034
```

In the above sample, the first line is correct since each code letter listed has the correct corresponding number.

On the second line, an error exists because code letter L should have the number 2 instead of the number 1.

On the third line, an error exists because the code letter S should have the number 7 instead of the number 5.

Since there are errors on two of the three lines, the correct answer is B.

1.	XMWBHLR	1358924	1. ...
	FWSLRHX	0572491	
	MTXBLTS	3618267	
2.	XTLSMRF	1627340	2. ...
	BMHRFLT	8394026	
	HLTSWRX	9267451	
3.	LMBSFXS	2387016	3. ...
	RWLMBSX	4532871	
	SMFXBHW	7301894	
4.	RSTWTSML	47657632	4. ...
	LXRMHFBS	21439087	
	FTLBMRWX	06273451	
5.	XSRSBWFM	17478603	5. ...
	BRMXRMXT	84314216	
	XSTFBWRL	17609542	
6.	TMSBXHLS	63781927	6. ...
	RBSFLFWM	48702053	
	MHFXWTRS	39015647	

―

TEST 3

DIRECTIONS FOR THIS SECTION: Questions 1 through 5 consist of three lines of code letters and numbers. The numbers on each line should correspond with the code letters on the same line in accordance with the table below.

Code Letter	P	L	I	J	B	O	H	U	C	G
Corresponding Number	0	1	2	3	4	5	6	7	8	9

On some of the lines, an error exists in the coding. Compare the letters and numbers in each question carefully. If you find an error or errors on

> only *one* of the lines in the question, mark your answer A;
> any *two* lines in the question, mark your answer B;
> all *three* lines in the question, mark your answer C;
> *none* of the lines in the question, mark your answer D.

3

SAMPLE QUESTION

JHOILCP	3652180
BICLGUP	4286970
UCIBHLJ	5824613

In the above sample, the first line is correct since each code letter listed has the correct corresponding number.

On the second line, an error exists because code letter L should have the number 1 instead of the number 6.

On the third line an error exists because the code letter U should have the number 7 instead of the number 5.

Since there are errors on two of the three lines, the correct answer is B.

1.	BULJCIP	4713920	1.	...
	HIGPOUL	6290571		
	OCUHJBI	5876342		
2.	CUBLOIJ	8741023	2.	...
	LCLGCLB	1818914		
	JPUHIOC	3076158		
3.	OIJGCBPO	52398405	3.	...
	UHPBLIOP	76041250		
	CLUIPGPC	81720908		
4.	BPCOUOJI	40875732	4.	...
	UOHCIPLB	75682014		
	GLHUUCBJ	92677843		
5.	HOIOHJLH	65256361	5.	...
	IOJJHHBP	25536640		
	OJHBJOPI	53642502		

TEST 4

DIRECTIONS FOR THIS SECTION: Questions 1 through 5 consist of three lines of code letters and numbers. The numbers on each line should correspond with the code letters on the same line in accordance with the table below.

Code Letters	Q	S	L	Y	M	O	U	N	W	Z
Corresponding Numbers	1	2	3	4	5	6	7	8	9	0

On some of the lines, an error exists in the coding. Compare the letters and numbers in each question carefully. If you find an error on

only *one* of the lines in the question, mark your answer A;
any *two* lines in the question, mark your answer B;
all *three* lines in the question, mark your answer C;
none of the lines in the question, mark your answer D.

SAMPLE QUESTION

MOQNWZQS	56189012
QWNMOLYU	19865347
LONLMYWN	36835489

In the above sample, the first line is correct since each code letter, as listed, has the correct corresponding number.

On the second line, an error exists because code letter M should have the number 5 instead of the number 6.

On the third line an error exists because the code letter W should have the number 9 instead of the number 8.

Since there are errors on two of the three lines, the correct answer is B.

1.	SMUWOLQN	25796318	1. ...
	ULSQNMZL	73218503	
	NMYQZUSL	85410723	
2.	YUWWMYQZ	47995410	2. ...
	SOSOSQSO	26262126	
	ZUNLWMYW	07839549	
3.	QULSWZYN	17329045	3. ...
	ZYLQWOYW	04319639	.
	QLUYWZSO	13749026	
4.	NLQZOYUM	83106475	4. ...
	SQMUWZOM	21579065	
	MMYWMZSQ	55498021	
5.	NQLOWZZU	81319007	5. ...
	SMYLUNZO	25347806	
	UWMSNZOL	79528013	

TEST 5

DIRECTIONS FOR THIS SECTION: Answer Questions 1 through 6 *SOLELY* on the basis of the chart and the instructions given below.

Toll Rate	$.25	$.30	$.45	$.60	$.75	$.90	$1.20	$2.50
Classification Number of Vehicle	1	2	3	4	5	6	7	8

Assume that each of the amounts of money on the above chart is a toll rate charged for a type of vehicle and that the number immediately below each amount is the classification number for that type of vehicle. For instance, "1" is the classification number for a vehicle paying a $.25 toll; "2" is the classification number for a vehicle paying a $.30 toll; and so forth.

In each question, a series of tolls is given in Column I. Column II gives four different arrangements of classification numbers. You are to pick the answer (A, B, C, or D) in Column II that gives the classification numbers that match the tolls in Column I and are in the same order as the tolls in Column I.

SAMPLE QUESTION

Column I | Column II
$.30, $.90, $2.50, $.45 | A. 2, 6, 8, 2
| B. 2, 8, 6, 3
| C. 2, 6, 8, 3
| D. 1, 6, 8, 3

5

According to the chart, the classification numbers that correspond to these toll rates are as follows: $.30 - 2, $.90 - 6, $2.50 - 8, $.45 - 3. Therefore, the right answer is 2, 6, 8, 3. The answer is C in Column II.

Do the following questions in the same way.

	Column I	Column II	
1.	$.60, $.30, $.90, $1.20, $.60	A. 4, 6, 2, 8, 4 B. 4, 2, 6, 7, 4 C. 2, 4, 7, 6, 2 D. 2, 4, 6, 7, 4	1. ...
2.	$.90, $.45, $.25, $.45, $2.50, $.75	A. 6, 3, 1, 3, 8, 3 B. 6, 3, 3, 1, 8, 5 C. 6, 1, 3, 3, 8, 5 D. 6, 3, 1, 3, 8, 5	2. ...
3.	$.45, $.75, $1.20, $.25, $.25, $.30, $.45	A. 3, 5, 7, 1, 1, 2, 3 B. 5, 3, 7, 1, 1, 2, 3 C. 3, 5, 7, 1, 2, 1, 3 D. 3, 7, 5, 1, 1, 2, 3	3. ...
4.	$1.20, $2.50, $.45, $.90, $1.20, $.75, $.25	A. 7, 8, 5, 6, 7, 5, 1 B. 7, 8, 3, 7, 6, 5, 1 C. 7, 8, 3, 6, 7, 5, 1 D. 7, 8, 3, 6, 7, 1, 5	4. ...
5.	$2.50, $1.20, $.90, $.25, $.60, $.45, $.30	A. 8, 6, 7, 1, 4, 3, 2 B. 8, 7, 5, 1, 4, 3, 2 C. 8, 7, 6, 2, 4, 3, 2 D. 8, 7, 6, 1, 4, 3, 2	5. ...
6.	$.75, $.25, $.45, $.60, $.90, $.30, $2.50	A. 5, 1, 3, 2, 4, 6, 8 B. 5, 1, 3, 4, 2, 6, 8 C. 5, 1, 3, 4, 6, 2, 8 D. 5, 3, 1, 4, 6, 2, 8	6. ...

TEST 6

DIRECTIONS FOR THIS SECTION: Answer Questions 1 through 10 on the basis of the following information:

A code number for any item is obtained by combining the date of delivery, number of units received, and number of units used.

The first two digits represent the day of the month, the third and fourth digits represent the month, and the fifth and sixth digits represent the year.

The number following the letter R represents the number of units received and the number following the letter U represents the number of units used.

For example, the code number 120673-R5690-U1001 indicates that a delivery of 5,690 units was made on June 12, 1973 of which 1,001 units were used.

Questions 1-6.
DIRECTIONS: Using the chart below, answer Questions 1 through 6 by choosing the letter (A, B, C, or D) in which the supplier and stock number correspond to the code number given.

Supplier	Stock Number	Number of Units Received	Delivery Date	Number of Units Used
Stony	38390	8300	May 11, 1972	3800
Stoney	39803	1780	September 15, 1973	1703
Nievo	21220	5527	October 10, 1973	5007
Nieve	38903	1733	August 5, 1973	1703
Monte	39213	5527	October 10, 1972	5007
Stony	38890	3308	December 9, 1972	3300
Stony	83930	3880	September 12, 1972	380
Nevo	47101	485	June 11, 1972	231
Nievo	12122	5725	May 11, 1973	5201
Neve	47101	9721	August 15, 1973	8207
Nievo	21120	2275	January 7, 1972	2175
Rosa	41210	3821	March 3, 1973	2710
Stony	38890	3308	September 12, 1972	3300
Dinal	54921	1711	April 2, 1973	1117
Stony	33890	8038	March 5, 1973	3300
Dinal	54721	1171	March 2, 1972	717
Claridge	81927	3308	April 5, 1973	3088
Nievo	21122	4878	June 7, 1972	3492
Haley	39670	8300	December 23, 1973	5300

1. Code No. 120972-R3308-U3300   1. ...
   A. Nievo - 12122   B. Stony - 83930
   C. Nievo - 21220   D. Stony - 38890
2. Code No. 101072-R5527-U5007   2. ...
   A. Nievo - 21220   B. Haley - 39670
   C. Monte - 39213   D. Claridge - 81927
3. Code No. 101073-R5527-U5007   3. ...
   A. Nievo - 21220   B. Monte - 39213
   C. Nievo - 12122   D. Nievo - 21120
4. Code No. 110573-R5725-U5201   4. ...
   A. Nievo - 12122   B. Nievo - 21220
   C. Haley - 39670   D. Stony - 38390
5. Code No. 070172-R2275-U2175   5. ...
   A. Stony - 33890   B. Stony - 83930
   C. Stony - 38390   D. Nievo - 21120
6. Code No. 120972-R3880-U380   6. ...
   A. Stony - 83930   B. Stony - 38890
   C. Stony - 33890   D. Monte - 39213

Questions 7-10.
DIRECTIONS: Using the same chart, answer Questions 7 through 10 by choosing the letter (A, B, C, or D) in which the code number corresponds to the supplier and stock number given.
7. Nieve - 38903   7. ...
   A. 851973-R1733-U1703   B. 080572-R1733-U1703
   C. 080573-R1733-U1703   D. 050873-R1733-U1703

8. Nevo - 47101
    A. 081573-R9721-U8207   B. 091573-R9721-U8207
    C. 110672-R485-U231   D. 061172-R485-U231
9. Dinal - 54921
    A. 020473-R1711-U1117   B. 030272-R1171-U717
    C. 020372-R1171-U717   D. 421973-R1711-U1117
10. Nievo - 21122
    A. 070672-R4878-U3492   B. 060772-R4878-U349
    C. 761972-R4878-U3492   D. 060772-R4878-U3492

8. ...

9. ...

10. ...

KEYS (CORRECT ANSWERS)

TEST 1	TEST 2	TEST 3
1. D	1. D	1. A
2. B	2. A	2. C
3. A	3. C	3. D
4. C	4. B	4. B
5. C	5. C	5. C
6. A	6. D	
7. D		
8. B		
9. D		
10. A		

TEST 4	TEST 5	TEST 6
1. D	1. B	1. D
2. D	2. D	2. C
3. B	3. A	3. A
4. A	4. C	4. A
5. C	5. D	5. D
	6. C	6. A
		7. D
		8. C
		9. A
		10. A

8

BASIC FUNDAMENTALS OF BOOKKEEPING

I. INTRODUCTION

Why keep records? If you are a typical small-business man, your answer to this question is probably, "Because the Government requires it!" And if the question comes in the middle of a busy day, you may add a few heartfelt words about the amount of time you have to spend on records--just for the Government.

Is it "just for the Government," though? True, regulations of various governmental agencies have greatly increased the record-keeping requirements of business. But this may be a good thing for the small-business man, overburdened though he is.

Many small-business managers don't recognize their book-keeping records for what they can really do. Their attitudes concerning these records are typified by one businessman who said, "Records only tell you what you have done in the past. It's too late to do anything about the past; I need to know what is going to happen in the future." However, the past can tell us much about what may happen in the future; and, certainly we can profit in the future from knowledge of our past mistakes.

These same managers may recognize that records are necessary in filing their tax returns, or that a banker requires financial information before he will lend money, but often their appreciation of their bookkeeping systems ends at this point. However, there are many ways in which the use of such information can help an owner manage his business more easily and profitably.

The small-business man is confronted with an endless array of problems and decisions every day. Sound decisions require an informed manager; and many management problems can be solved with the aid of the right bookkeeping information.

II. Requirements of a Good Record System

Of course, to get information that is really valuable to you--to get the right information--requires a good bookkeeping system. What are the characteristics of a good system? You want one that is simple and easy to understand, reliable, accurate, consistent, and one that will get the information to you promptly.

A simple, well-organized system of records, regularly kept up, can actually be a timesaver--by bringing order out of disorder. Furthermore, competition is very strong in today's business areas. A businessman needs to know almost on a day-to-day basis where his business stands profitwise, which lines of merchandise or services are the most or the least profitable, what his working-capital needs are, and many other details. He can get this information with reasonable certainty only if he has a good recordkeeping system--one that gives him all the information he needs.

In setting up a recordkeeping system that is tailored to your business, you will probably need the professional help of a competent accountant. And you may want to retain the services of an accountant or bookkeeper to maintain these records. But it is your job to learn to interpret this information and to use it effectively.

One of the reasons that many managers have misgivings about keeping records is that they don't understand them or know how they can be used. The owner or manager of a small business may be an expert in his line of business; however, he generally does not have a background in keeping records. So he is usually confused. What we will try to do in this discussion is to highlight the "why and what of bookkeeping." In so-doing, we aim to eliminate that confusion.

III. IMPORTANT BOOKKEEPING RECORDS

Today's managers should be familiar with the following book-keeping records:

Journal

Ledgers

Balance sheet

Income statement

Funds flow statement

We will discuss each of them in turn. In addition, a brief discussion of other supporting records will be made.

A. Bookkeeping Books

The journal, which accountants call "the book of original entry," is a chronological record of all business transactions engaged in by the firm. It is simply a financial diary. The ledgers, or "books of account," are more specialized records used to classify the journal entries according to like elements. For example, there would be a separate ledger account for cash entries, another for all sales, and still others for items such as accounts receivable, inventory, and loans. All transactions are first entered in the journal, and then posted in the appropriate ledger. The journal and ledgers are of minor importance to the manager in making decisions, but they play a vital role for the accountant or bookkeeper because the more important accounting statements such as the balance sheet and the income statement are derived from the journal and ledger entries.

3

B. Financial Reports

The two principal financial reports in most businesses are the balance sheet and the income statement. Up to about 25 or 30 years ago, the balance sheet was generally considered to be the most important financial statement. Until that time, it was generally used only as a basis for the extension of credit and bank loans, and very little thought was given to the information it offered that might be important in the operation and management of the business. Starting about 30 years ago, emphasis has gradually shifted to the income statement. Today the balance sheet and income statements are of equal importance, both to the accountant in financial reporting and to the manager faced with a multitude of administrative problems.

Essentially, the balance sheet shows what a business has, what it owes, and the investment of the owners in the business. It can be likened to a snapshot, showing the financial condition of the business at a certain point in time. The income statement, on the other hand, is a summary of business operations for a certain period--usually between two balance sheet dates. The income statement can be compared to a moving picture; it indicates the activity of a business over a certain period of time. In very general terms, the balance sheet tells you where you are, and the income statement tells you how you got there since the last time you had a balance sheet prepared.

Both the balance sheet and income statement can be long and complicated documents. Both accountants and management need some device that can highlight the critical financial information contained in these complex documents. Certain standard ratios or relationships between items on the financial statements have been developed that allow the interested parties to quickly determine important characteristics of the firm's activities. There are many relationships that might be important in a specific business that would not be as significant in another.

Other devices of the bookkeeper, such as funds flow statements, daily summaries of sales and cash receipts, the checkbook, account receivable records, property depreciation records, and insurance scheduling have also been found useful to management.

C. THE BALANCE SHEET

As stated earlier, the balance sheet represents what a business has, what it owes, and the investment of the owners. The things of value that the business has or owns are called <u>assets.</u> The claims of creditors against these assets are called <u>liabilities.</u> The value of the assets over and above the liabilities can be justifiably called the owner's claim. This amount is usually called the <u>owner's equity</u> (or net worth).

This brings us to the <u>dual-aspect concept</u> of bookkeeping. The balance sheet is set up to portray two aspects of each entry or event recorded on it. For each thing of value, or asset, there is a claim against that asset. The recognition of this concept leads to the balance sheet formula: ASSETS = LIABILITIES + OWNER'S EQUITY. Let's take an example to clarify this concept. Suppose Joe Smith decides to start a business. He has $2,000 cash in the bank. He got this sum by investing $1,000 of his own money and by borrowing $1,000 from the bank. If he were to draw up a balance sheet at this time, he would have assets of $2,000 cash balanced against a liability claim of $1,000 and an owner's claim of $1,000. Using the balance sheet

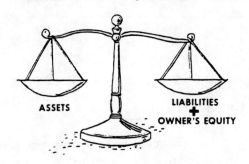

ASSETS = LIABILITIES + OWNER'S EQUITY

ASSETS

LIABILITIES
+
OWNER'S EQUITY

Visual No. 2

formula: $2,000 = $1,000 + $1,000. This formula means there will always be a balance between assets and claims against them. The balance sheet <u>always</u> balances unless there has been a clerical error.

THE BLANK COMPANY
December 31, 196-

ASSETS

LIABILITIES

OWNER'S EQUITY

Visual No. 3

The balance sheet is usually constructed in a two-column format. The assets appear in the left hand column and the claims against the assets (the liabilities and owner's equity) are in the right hand column. Other formats are sometimes used; but, in any case, the balance sheet is an itemized or detailed account of the basic formula: assets = liabilities + owner's equity.

5

1. Assets

I have been speaking of assets belonging to the business. Of course, the business does not legally own anything unless it is organized as a corporation. But regardless of whether the business is organized as a proprietorship, a partnership, or a corporation, all business bookkeeping should be reckoned and accounted apart from the accounting of the personal funds and assets of its owners.

Assets are typically classified into three categories:

Current assets

Fixed assets

Other assets

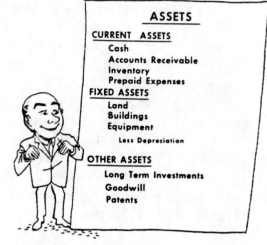

ASSETS

CURRENT ASSETS
  Cash
  Accounts Receivable
  Inventory
  Prepaid Expenses
FIXED ASSETS
  Land
  Buildings
  Equipment
    Less Depreciation
OTHER ASSETS
  Long Term Investments
  Goodwill
  Patents

a. Current Assets

Visual No. 4

For bookkeeping purposes, the term "current assets" is used to designate cash and other assets which can be converted to cash during the normal operating cycle of the business (usually one year). The distinction between current assets and noncurrent assets is important since lenders and others pay much attention to the total amount of current assets. The size of current assets has a significant relationship to the stability of the business because it represents, to some degree, the amount of cash that might be raised quickly to meet current obligations. Here are some of the major current asset items.

Cash consists of funds that are immediately available to use without restrictions. These funds are usually in the form of checking-account deposits in banks, cash-register money, and petty cash. Cash should be large enough to meet obligations that are immediately due.

Accounts receivable are amounts owed to the company by its customers as a result of sales. Essentially, these accounts are the result of granting credit to customers. They may take the form of charge accounts where no interest or service charge is made, or they may be of an interest-bearing nature. In either case they are a drain on working capital. The more that is outstanding on accounts receivable, the less money that is available to meet current needs. The trick with accounts receivable is to keep them small enough so as not to endanger working capital, but large enough to keep from losing sales to credit-minded customers.

Inventory is defined as those items which are held for sale in the ordinary course of business, or which are to be consumed in the production of goods and services that are to be sold. Since accountants are conservative by nature, they include in inventory only items that are salable, and these items are valued at cost or market value, whichever is lower. Control of inventory and inventory expenses is one of management's most important jobs-- particularly for retailers--and good bookkeeping records in this area are particularly useful.

Prepaid expenses represent assets, paid for in advance, but whose usefulness will usually expire in a short time. A good example of this is prepaid insurance. A business pays for insurance protection in advance--usually three to five years in advance. The right to this protection is a thing of value--an asset--and the unused portion can be refunded or converted to cash.

b. Fixed Assets

"Fixed assets" are items owned by the business that have relatively long life. These assets are used in the production or sale of other goods and services. If they were held for resale, they would be classified as inventory, even though they might be long-lived assets.

Normally these assets are composed of land, buildings, and equipment. Some companies lump their fixed assets into one entry on their balance sheets, but you gain more information and can exercise more control over these assets if they are listed separately on the balance sheet. You may even want to list various types of equipment separately.

There is one other aspect of fixed-asset bookkeeping that we should discuss--and this is depreciation. Generally fixed assets--with the exception of land--depreciate, or decrease in value with the passing of time. That is, a building or piece of equipment that is five years old is not worth as much as it was when it was new. For a balance sheet to show the true value of these assets, it must reflect this loss in value. For both tax and other accounting purposes, the businessman is allowed to deduct this loss in value each year over the useful life of the assets, until, over a period of time, he has deducted the total cost of the asset. There are several accepted ways to calculate how much of an asset's value can be deducted for depreciation in a given year. This information and other facts concerning depreciation are discussed in Small Marketers Aid No. 68, Depreciation Costs - Don't Overlook Them, which is available free from the SBA. (See Supply Department.) Depreciation is allowed as an expense item on the income statement, and we will discuss this fact later.

c. Other Assets

"Other assets" is a miscellaneous category. It accounts for any investments of the firm in securities, such as stock in other private companies or government bonds. It also includes intangible assets such as goodwill, patents, and franchise costs. Items in the "other-assets" category have a longer life than current-asset items.

2. Liabilities

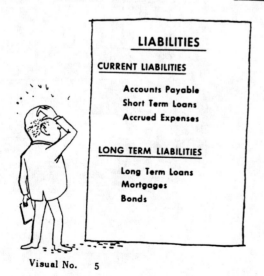

LIABILITIES

CURRENT LIABILITIES

Accounts Payable
Short Term Loans
Accrued Expenses

LONG TERM LIABILITIES

Long Term Loans
Mortgages
Bonds

Visual No. 5

"Liabilities" are the amounts of money owed by the business to people other than the owners. They are claims against the company's total assets, although they are not claims against any specific asset, except in the cases of some mortgages and equipment liens. Essentially, liabilities are divided into two classes:

Current liabilities

Long-term liabilities.

a. Current Liabilities

The term "current liabilities" is used to describe those claims of outsiders on the business that will fall due within one year. Here are some of the more important current-liabilities entries on the balance sheet:

Accounts payable represent the amounts owed to vendors, wholesalers, and other suppliers from whom the business has bought items on account. This includes any items of inventory, supply, or capital equipment which have been purchased on credit and for which payment is expected in less than one year. For example, a retail butcher purchased 500 pounds of meat for $250, a quantity of fish that cost $50, and a new air-conditioning unit for his store for $450. He bought all of these items on 60-day terms. His accounts payable were increased by $750. Of course, at the same time his inventory increased by $300 and his fixed assets rose by $450. If he had paid cash for these items, his accounts payable would not have been affected, but his cash account would have decreased by $750, thus keeping the accounting equation in balance.

Short-term loans, which are sometimes called notes payable, are loans from individuals, banks, or other lending institutions which fall due within a year. Also included in this category is the portion of any long-term debt that will come due within a year.

Accrued expenses are obligations which the company has incurred, but for which there has been no formal bill or invoice as yet. An example of this is accrued taxes. The owner knows the business has the obligation to pay taxes; and they are accruing or accumulating each day. The fact that the taxes do not have to be paid until a later date

9

does not diminish the obligation. Another example of accrued expenses is wages. Although wages are paid weekly or monthly, they are being earned hourly or daily and constitute a valid claim against the company. An accurate balance sheet will reflect these obligations.

b. Long-Term Liabilities

Claims of outsiders on the business that do not come due within one year are called "long-term liabilities" or, simply, "other liabilities." Included in this category are bonded indebtedness, mortgages, and long-term loans from individuals, banks, and others from whom the business may borrow money, such as the SBA. As was stated before, any part of a long-term debt that falls due within one year from the date of the balance sheet would be recorded as part of the current liabilities of the business.

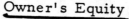

Owner's Equity

The owner's equity section of the balance sheet is located on the right-hand side underneath the listing of the liabilities. It shows the claims of the owners on the company. Essentially, this is a balancing figure--that is, the owners get what's left of the assets after the liability claims have been recognized. This is an obvious definition, if you will remember the balance sheet formula. Transposing the formula as we learned it a few minutes ago, it becomes Assets - Liabilities = Owner's Equity. In the case where the business is a sole proprietorship, it is customary to show owner's equity as one entry with no distinction being made between the owner's initial investment and the accumulated retained earnings of the business. However, in the case of an incorporated business, there are entries for stockholders' claims as well as for earnings that have been accumulated and retained in the business. Of course, if the business has been consistently operating at a loss, the proprietor's claim may be less than his initial investment. And, in the case of a corporation, the balancing account could be operating deficit rather than retained earnings.

If we put together the entries we have been talking about, we have a complete balance sheet (such as the one shown in Visual No. 6 for the Blank Company). There is a lot of information in this statement. It tells you just what you have and where it is. It also tells you what you owe. You need this information to help you decide what actions you should take in running your business. If you need to borrow money, the banker or anyone else from whom you borrow will want to look at your balance sheet.

BALANCE SHEET				
THE BLANK COMPANY				
December 31, 196-				
ASSETS			**LIABILITIES**	
CURRENT ASSETS			Accounts Payable	1,400
Cash		$ 1,200	Accrued Expenses	750
Accounts Receivable		2,500	Short Term Loans	1,000
Inventory		2,500		
			Long Term Loan	5,000
FIXED ASSETS			Mortgage	7,000
Land		3,000		
Building	15,000			
Equipment	2,500		**OWNER'S EQUITY**	
	17,500		John Q. Blank	5,000
Less			Earned Surplus	1,050
Depreciation	5,500	12,000		
		$21,200		$21,200

Visual No. 6

D. THE INCOME STATEMENT

In recent years the income statement has become as important as the balance sheet as a financial and management record. It is also called the profit and loss statement, or simply the P and L statement. This financial record summarizes the activities of the company over a period of time, listing those that can be expressed in dollars. That is, it reports the revenues of the company and the expenses incurred in obtaining the revenues, and it shows the profit or loss resulting from these activities. The income statement complements the balance sheet. While balance sheet analysis shows the change in position of the company at the end of accounting periods, the income statement shows how the change took place during the accounting period. Both reports are necessary for a full understanding of the operation of the business.

INCOME STATEMENT	
THE BLANK COMPANY	
January 1, 196- to December 31, 196-	
SALES	$50,000
COST OF GOODS SOLD	35,000
GROSS MARGIN	15,000
EXPENSES	13,400
PROFIT BEFORE TAXES	1,600
TAXES	400
NET PROFIT	$1,200

Visual No. 7

The income statement for a particular company should be tailored to fit the activities of that company, and there is no rigid format that must be followed in constructing this report. But the following categories are found in most income statements.

11

1. Sales

The major activity of most businesses is the sales of products and services, and the bulk of revenue comes from sales. In recording sales, the figure used is net sales--that is, sales after discounts, allowances, and returned goods have been accounted for.

2. Cost of Goods Sold

Another important item, in calculating profit or loss, is the cost of the goods that the company has sold. This item is difficult to calculate accurately. Since the goods sold come from inventory, and since the company may have bought parts of its inventory at several prices, it is hard to determine exactly what is the cost of the particular part of the inventory that was sold. In large companies, and particularly in companies using cost accounting, there are some rather complicated methods of determining "cost of goods sold," but they are beyond the scope of this presentation. However, there is a simple, generally accepted way of calculating cost of goods sold. In this method you simply add the net amount of purchases during the accounting period to your beginning inventory, and subtract from this your ending inventory. The result can be considered cost-of-goods sold.

COST OF GOODS SOLD

BEGINNING INVENTORY		$ 2,400
PURCHASES	+	35,100
GOODS AVAILABLE FOR SALE	=	37,500
ENDING INVENTORY	−	2,500
COST OF GOODS SOLD	=	$35,000

Visual No. 8

3. Gross Margin

The difference between sales and cost of goods sold is called the "gross margin" or gross profit. This item is often expressed as a percentage of sales, as well as in dollar figures. The percentage gross margin is a very significant figure because it indicates what the average markup is on the merchandise sold. So, if a manager knows his expenses as a percentage of sales, he can calculate the markup necessary to obtain the gross margin he needs for a profitable operation. It is surprising how many small-business men do not know what basis to use in setting markups. In fact, with the various allowances, discounts, and markdowns that a business may offer, many managers do not know what their markup actually is. The gross margin calculation on the income statement can help the manager with this problem.

12

There are other costs of running a business besides the cost of the goods sold. When you use the simple method of determining costs of goods sold, these costs are called "expenses."

For example, here are some typical expenses: salaries and wages, utilities, depreciation, interest, administrative expenses, supplies, bad debts, advertising, and taxes--Federal, State, and local. These

EXPENSES	
SALARIES & WAGES	$5,500
UTILITIES	500
DEPRECIATION	875
INTEREST	600
INSURANCE	100
ADMINISTRATIVE EXPENSE	5,000
SUPPLIES	125
BAD DEBT EXPENSE	100
ADVERTISING	250
STATE, LOCAL & EXCISE TAXES	350
TOTAL EXPENSES	$13,400

Visual No. 9

are typical expenses, but there are many other kinds of expenses that may be experienced by other businesses. For example, we have shown in the Blank Company's balance sheet that he owns his own land and building--with a mortgage, of course. This accounts for part of his depreciation and interest expenses, but for a company that rents its quarters, rent would appear as the expense item. Other common expenses are traveling expense, commissions, and advertising.

Most of these expense items are self-explanatory, but there are a few that merit further comment. For one thing, the salary or draw of the owner should be recorded among the expenses--either as a part of salaries and wages or as part of administrative expenses. To exclude the owner's compensation from expenses distorts the actual profitability of the business. And, if the company is incorporated, it would reduce the allowable tax deductions of the business. Of course, for tax purposes, the owner's salary or draw in a proprietorship or partnership is considered as part of the net profit.

We discussed depreciation when we examined the balance sheet, and we mentioned that it was an item of expense. Although no money is actually paid out for depreciation, it is a real expense because it represents reduction in the value of the assets.

The most important thing about expenses is to be sure to include all of the expenses that the business incurs. This not only helps the owner get a more accurate picture of his operation but it allows him to take full advantage of the tax deductions that legitimate expenses offer.

13

4. Net Profit

In a typical company, when expenses are subtracted from gross margin, the remainder is profit. However, if the business receives revenue from sources other than sales, such as rents, dividends on securities held by the company, or interest on money loaned by the company, it is added to profit at this point. For bookkeeping purposes, the resulting profit is labeled "profit before taxes." This is the figure from which Federal income taxes are figured. If the business is a proprietorship, the profit is taxed as part of the owner's income. If the business is a corporation, the profits may be taxed on the basis of the corporate income tax schedule. When income taxes have been accounted for, the resultant entry is called "net profit after taxes," or simply "net profit." This is usually the final entry on the income statement.

Another financial record which managers can use to advantage is the funds flow statement. This statement is also called statement of sources and uses of funds and sometimes the "where got--where gone" statement. Whatever you call it, a record of sources and uses of past funds is useful to the manager. He can use it to evaluate past performance, and as a guide in determining future uses and sources of money.

When we speak of "funds" we do not necessarily mean actual "dollars" or "cash." Although accounting records are all written in monetary terms, they do not always involve an exchange of money. Many times in business transactions, it is credit rather than dollars that changes hands. Therefore, when we speak of funds flow, we are speaking of exchanges of economic values rather than merely the physical flow of dollars.

Basically, funds are used to: increase assets and reduce liabilities. They are also sometimes used to reduce owner's equity. An example of this would be the use of company funds to buy up outstanding stock or to buy out a partner. Where do funds come from? The three basic sources of funds are a reduction in assets, increases in liabilities, and increased owner's equity. All balance sheet items can be affected by the obtaining and spending of company funds.

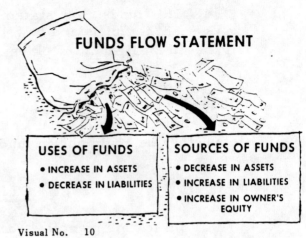

FUNDS FLOW STATEMENT

USES OF FUNDS	SOURCES OF FUNDS
• INCREASE IN ASSETS	• DECREASE IN ASSETS
• DECREASE IN LIABILITIES	• INCREASE IN LIABILITIES
	• INCREASE IN OWNER'S EQUITY

Visual No. 10

COMPARISON OF SELECTED BALANCE SHEET ITEMS
THE BLANK COMPANY

	LAST YEAR	THIS YEAR	SOURCE OF FUNDS	USE OF FUNDS
ASSETS				
CASH	1500	1200	300	
ACCOUNTS RECEIVABLE	2200	2500		300
INVENTORY	2300	2500		200
EQUIPMENT	2000	2500		500
LIABILITIES				
ACCOUNTS PAYABLE	1000	1400	400	
LONG TERM LOANS	5000	5000		
MORTGAGE	8000	7000		1000
OWNER'S EQUITY				
JOHN O. BLANK	4500	5000	500	
EARNED SURPLUS	250	1050	800	

Visual No. 11

To examine the construction and use of a funds flow statement, let's take another look at the Blank Company. Here we show comparative balance sheets for two one-year periods (Visual No. 12). For the sake of simplicity, we have included only selected items from the balance sheets for analysis. Notice that the company gained funds by:

reducing cash $300,

increasing accounts payable $400,

putting $500 more owner's equity in the business, and

plowing back $800 of the profit into the business.

These funds were used to:

increase accounts receivable $300,

increase inventory $200,

buy $500 worth of equipment, and

pay off $1,000 worth of long-term debt.

15

This funds flow statement has indicated to Mr. Blank where he has gotten his funds and how he has spent them. He can analyze these figures in the light of his plans and objectives and take appropriate action.

For example, if Mr. Blank wants to answer the question "Should I buy new capital equipment?" a look at his funds flow statement would show him his previous sources of funds, and it would give him a clue as to whether he could obtain funds for any new equipment.

IV. OTHER RECORDS

Up to this point, we have been talking about the basic types of bookkeeping records. In addition, we have discussed the two basic financial statements of a business: the balance sheet and the profit and loss statement. Now let us give our attention briefly to some other records which are very helpful to running a business successfully.

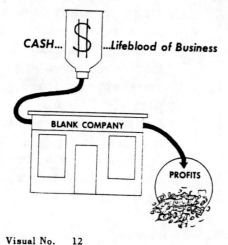

CASH... $ ...Lifeblood of Business

BLANK COMPANY

PROFITS

Visual No. 12

One element that appears on the balance sheet which I believe we can agree is important is cash. Because it is the lifeblood of all business, cash should be controlled and safeguarded at all times. The daily summary of sales and cash receipts and the checkbook are used by many managers of small businesses to help provide that control.

A. Daily Summary of Sales and Cash Receipts

Not all businesses summarize their daily transactions. However, a daily summary of sales and cash receipts is a very useful tool for checking how your business is doing on a day-to-day basis. At the close of each day's business, the actual cash on hand is counted and "balanced" against the total of the receipts recorded for the day. This balancing is done by means of the Daily Summary of Sales and Cash Receipts. (Handout No. 4-3). This is a recording of every cash receipt and every charge sale, whether you use a cash register or sales checks or both. If you have more than one cash register, a daily summary should be prepared for each; the individual cash-register summaries can then be combined into one overall summary for convenience in handling.

In the daily summary form used for purposes of illustration, (see Handout), the first section, "Cash Receipts," records the total of all cash taken in during the day from whatever source. This is the cash that must be accounted for over and above the amount in the change and/ or petty cash funds. We shall touch upon these two funds later. The three components of cash receipts are (1) cash sales, (2) collections on accounts, and (3) miscellaneous receipts.

The daily total of cash sales is obtained from a cash-register tape reading or, if no cash register is used, by totaling the cash-sales checks.

For collections on accounts, an individual record of each customer payment on account should be kept, whether or not these collections are rung up on a cash register. The amount to be entered on the daily summary is obtained by totaling these individual records.

Miscellaneous receipts are daily cash transactions that cannot be classified as sales or collections. They might include refunds from suppliers for overpayment, advertising rebates or allowances, collections of rent from sub-leases or concessions, etc. Like collections on account, a sales check or memo should be made out each time such cash is taken in.

The total of daily cash receipts to be accounted for on the daily summary is obtained by adding cash sales, collections on account, and miscellaneous receipts.

The second section, "Cash on Hand," of a daily summary is a count of the cash actually on hand plus the cash that is represented by petty cash slips. The daily summary provides for counts of your total coins, bills, and checks as well as the amount expended for petty cash. The latter is determined by adding the amounts on the individual petty cash slips. By totaling all four of these counts, you obtain the total cash accounted for. To determine the amount of your daily cash deposit, you deduct from the "total cash accounted for" the total of the petty cash and change funds.

Cash to be deposited on the daily summary should always equal the total receipts to be accounted for minus the fixed amount of your petty cash and change funds. If it does not, all the work in preparing the daily summary should be carefully checked. Obviously, an error in giving change, in ringing up a sale, or neglecting to do so, will result in a cash shortage or overage. The daily summary provides spaces for such errors so that the proper entries can be made in your bookkeeping records. The last section of your daily summary, "Sales," records the total daily sales broken down into (1) cash sales and (2) charge sales.

As soon as possible after the daily summary has been completed, all cash for deposit should be taken to the bank. A duplicate deposit slip, stamped by the bank, should be kept with the daily summary as evidence that the deposit was made.

B. Petty Cash and Charge Funds

The record of daily sales and cash receipts which we have just described is designed on the assumption that a petty cash fund and a change cash fund, or a combination change and petty cash fund, are used. All businesses, small and large, have day-to-day expenses that are so small they do not warrant the drawing of a check. Good management practice calls for careful control of such expenses. The petty cash fund provides such control. It is a sum of money which is obtained by drawing a check to provide several day's, a week's, or a month's need of cash for small purchases. The type of business will determine the amount of the petty cash fund.

DOCUMENT YOUR PETTY CASH EXPENSES

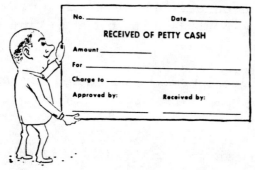

Visual No. 13

Each time a payment is made from the petty cash, a slip should be made out. If an invoice or receipt is available, it should be attached to the petty-cash slip. The slips and the money ordinarily, but not necessarily, are kept separate from other currency in your cash till, drawer, or register. At all times, the total of unspent petty cash and petty cash slips should equal the fixed amount of the fund. When the total of the slips approaches the fixed amount of the petty cash fund, a check is drawn for the total amount of the slips. The money from this check is used to bring the fund back to its fixed amount.

In addition to a petty cash fund, some businesses that receive cash in over-the-counter transactions have a change fund. The amount needed for making change varies with the size and type of business, and, in some cases, with the days of the week. Control of the money in your change fund will be made easier, however, if you set a fixed amount large enough to meet all the ordinary change-making needs of your business. Each day, when the day's receipts are balanced and prepared for a bank deposit, you will retain bills and coins totaling the fixed amount of the fund for use the following day. Since you had that amount on hand before you made the day's first sale, the entire amount of the day's receipts will still be available for your bank deposit.

18

In some cases, the petty cash fund is kept in a petty cash box or safe, apart from the change fund. However, the same fund can serve for both petty cash and change. For example, if you decide that you need $50 for making change and $25 for petty cash, one $75 fund can be used. Whenever, in balancing the day's operations, you see that the petty cash slips total more than $25, you can write a petty cash check for the amount of the slips.

C. Record of Cash Disbursement

To safeguard your cash, it is recommended that all receipts be deposited in a bank account and that all disbursements, except those made from the petty cash fund, be made by drawing a check on that account. Your bank account should be used exclusively for business transactions. If your business is typical, you will have to write checks for merchandise purchases, employee's salaries, rent, utilities, payroll taxes, petty cash, and various other expenses. Your check stubs will serve as a record of cash disbursements.

The checkbook stub should contain all the details of the disbursement including the date, payee, amount and purpose of the payment. In addition, a running balance of the amount you have in your bank account should be maintained by subtracting the amount of each check from the existing balance after the previous check was drawn. If the checks of your checkbook are prenumbered, it is important to mark plainly in the stub when a check is voided for one reason or another.

Each check should have some sort of written document to support it--an invoice, petty-cash voucher, payroll summary and so on. Supporting documents should be approved by you or someone you have authorized before a check is drawn. They should be marked paid and filed after the check is drawn.

Periodically, your bank will send you a statement of your account and return cancelled checks for which money has been withdrawn from your account. It is important that you reconcile your records with those of the bank. This means that the balances in your checkbook and on the bank statement should agree. Uncashed checks must be deducted from your checkbook balance and deposits not recorded on the bank statement must be added to its balance in order to get both balances to agree.

D. Accounts Receivable Records

If you extend credit to your customers, you must keep an accurate account of your credit sales not only in total as you have done on the daily summary but also by the amount that each individual customer owes you. Moreover, you must be systematic about billings and collections. This is important. It results in better relations with your charge customers and in fewer losses from bad debts.

The simplest method of handling accounts receivable--other than just keeping a file of sales-slip carbons--is to have an account sheet for each credit customer. Charge sales and payments on charge sales are posted to each customer sheet. Monthly billing to each of your charge customers should be made from their individual account sheets.

ACCOUNTS RECEIVABLE AGING SCHEDULE THE BLANK COMPANY							
CUSTOMER	TOTAL AMOUNT	CURRENT	30-60 DAYS	60-90 DAYS	3-7 MONTHS	7-12 MONTHS	OVER 1 YEAR
JOHN JONES	103 50	52 50	49 50				
SAM SMITH	23 00	23 00					
RICHARD ROE	9 75				9 75		
DAVID DOE	28 00	20 00			8 00		
JAMES JOHNSON	14 50					14 50	
WILLIAM WILLIAMS	35 00						35 00
TOTAL	450 00	336 50	72 75	5 00	16 00	5 00	10 00
PERCENT	100	75	16	1	4	1	2

Visual No. 14

At least two or three times a year, your accounts receivable should be aged. You do this by posting each customer's account and his unpaid charges in columns according to age. These columns are labeled: not due; 1 to 30 days past due; 31 to 60 days past due; 61 to 90 days past due; etc. This analysis will indicate those customers who are not complying with your credit terms.

E. Property Records and Depreciation

In every type of business, it is necessary to purchase property and equipment from time to time. This property usually will last for several years, so it would be unrealistic to show the total amount of the purchase as an expense in any one year. Therefore, when this property is set up in the books as an asset, records must be kept to decrease its value over its life. This decrease is known as depreciation. I have mentioned this before during this talk. The amount of the decrease in value in one year, that is, the depreciation, is charged as an expense for the year.

I am talking about this expense, particularly, because no cash is paid out for it. It is a non-cash, not-out-of-pocket expense. You don't have to hand over actual money at the end of the month.

Records should be kept of this because, otherwise, there is a danger that this expense will be overlooked. Yet it is impossible to figure true profit or loss without considering it.

When you deduct the depreciation expense from your firm's income, you reduce your tax liabilities. When you put this depreciation expense into a depreciation allowance account, you are keeping score on your "debt" to depreciation.

In a barber shop, to take a simple example, depreciation of its chairs, dryers, and clippers at the end of the year amounts to $136. You deduct this $136 from the shop's income, in this case, to pay the debt credited to your depreciation allowance account. Since this equipment has the same depreciation value each year, the depreciation allowance account at the end of 3 years will show that a total of $408 worth of equipment has been used up. The books of the barbershop therefore show an expense of $408 which actually has not been spent. It is in the business to replace the depreciated equipment. If replacement will not take place in the immediate future, the money can be used in inventory, or in some other way to generate more sales or profits.

How you handle this money depends on many things. You can set it aside at a low interest rate and have that much less operating money. Or you can put it to work in your business where it will help to keep your finances healthy.

Remember, however, that you must be prepared financially when it is time to buy replacement equipment. A depreciation allowance account on your books can help to keep you aware of this. It helps you keep score on how much depreciation or replacement money you are using in your business.

Keeping score with a depreciation allowance account helps you to know when you need to convert some of your assets into replacement cash. If, for example, you know on January 1 that your delivery truck will be totally depreciated by June 30, you can review the situation objectively. You can decide whether you ought to use the truck longer or replace it. If you decide to replace it, then you can plan to accumulate the cash, and time the purchase in order to make the best deal.

F. Schedule of Insurance Coverage

The schedule of insurance coverage is prepared to indicate the type of coverage and the amount presently in force. This schedule should list all the insurance carried by your business--fire and extended coverage, theft, liability, life, business interruption and so forth.

This schedule should be prepared to present the following: name of insurance company, annual premium, expiration date, type of coverage, amount of coverage, asset insured, and estimated current value of asset insured.

An analysis of this schedule should indicate the adequacy of insurance coverage. A review of this schedule with your insurance agent is suggested.

V. CONCLUSION

During the brief time allotted to this subject of the basic fundamentals of bookkeeping, we have just scratched its surface. What we have tried to do is to inform you, as small-business managers, of the importance of good records. We have described the components of the important records that you must have if you are going to manage your business efficiently and profitably. In addition, we have brought to your attention some of the subsidiary records that will aid you in managing your business.

There are other records such as breakeven charts, budgets, cost accounting systems, to mention a few, which can also benefit the progressive manager. However, we do not have the time even to give you the highlights of those management tools. Your accountant can assist you in learning to understand and use them. Moreover, he can help you to develop and use the records we have discussed. For further information about them, you also can read the publications of the Small Business Administration, some of which are available to you free of charge. By reading and using the accounting advice available to you, you can make sure that you have the right records to improve your managing skill and thereby increase your profits.

ANSWER SHEET

USE THE SPECIAL PENCIL.   MAKE GLOSSY BLACK MARKS.

1 A B C D E	26 A B C D E	51 A B C D E	76 A B C D E	101 A B C D E
2 A B C D E	27 A B C D E	52 A B C D E	77 A B C D E	102 A B C D E
3 A B C D E	28 A B C D E	53 A B C D E	78 A B C D E	103 A B C D E
4 A B C D E	29 A B C D E	54 A B C D E	79 A B C D E	104 A B C D E
5 A B C D E	30 A B C D E	55 A B C D E	80 A B C D E	105 A B C D E
6 A B C D E	31 A B C D E	56 A B C D E	81 A B C D E	106 A B C D E
7 A B C D E	32 A B C D E	57 A B C D E	82 A B C D E	107 A B C D E
8 A B C D E	33 A B C D E	58 A B C D E	83 A B C D E	108 A B C D E
9 A B C D E	34 A B C D E	59 A B C D E	84 A B C D E	109 A B C D E
10 A B C D E	35 A B C D E	60 A B C D E	85 A B C D E	110 A B C D E

Make only ONE mark for each answer.   Additional and stray marks may be
counted as mistakes.   In making corrections, erase errors COMPLETELY.

11 A B C D E	36 A B C D E	61 A B C D E	86 A B C D E	111 A B C D E
12 A B C D E	37 A B C D E	62 A B C D E	87 A B C D E	112 A B C D E
13 A B C D E	38 A B C D E	63 A B C D E	88 A B C D E	113 A B C D E
14 A B C D E	39 A B C D E	64 A B C D E	89 A B C D E	114 A B C D E
15 A B C D E	40 A B C D E	65 A B C D E	90 A B C D E	115 A B C D E
16 A B C D E	41 A B C D E	66 A B C D E	91 A B C D E	116 A B C D E
17 A B C D E	42 A B C D E	67 A B C D E	92 A B C D E	117 A B C D E
18 A B C D E	43 A B C D E	68 A B C D E	93 A B C D E	118 A B C D E
19 A B C D E	44 A B C D E	69 A B C D E	94 A B C D E	119 A B C D E
20 A B C D E	45 A B C D E	70 A B C D E	95 A B C D E	120 A B C D E
21 A B C D E	46 A B C D E	71 A B C D E	96 A B C D E	121 A B C D E
22 A B C D E	47 A B C D E	72 A B C D E	97 A B C D E	122 A B C D E
23 A B C D E	48 A B C D E	73 A B C D E	98 A B C D E	123 A B C D E
24 A B C D E	49 A B C D E	74 A B C D E	99 A B C D E	124 A B C D E
25 A B C D E	50 A B C D E	75 A B C D E	100 A B C D E	125 A B C D E

ANSWER SHEET

TEST NO. _____ PART _____ TITLE OF POSITION _____

PLACE OF EXAMINATION _____ DATE _____

(CITY OR TOWN)   (STATE)

RATING

USE THE SPECIAL PENCIL.   MAKE GLOSSY BLACK MARKS.

#	A B C D E	#	A B C D E	#	A B C D E	#	A B C D E	#	A B C D E
1	:: :: :: :: ::	26	:: :: :: :: ::	51	:: :: :: :: ::	76	:: :: :: :: ::	101	:: :: :: :: ::
2	:: :: :: :: ::	27	:: :: :: :: ::	52	:: :: :: :: ::	77	:: :: :: :: ::	102	:: :: :: :: ::
3	:: :: :: :: ::	28	:: :: :: :: ::	53	:: :: :: :: ::	78	:: :: :: :: ::	103	:: :: :: :: ::
4	:: :: :: :: ::	29	:: :: :: :: ::	54	:: :: :: :: ::	79	:: :: :: :: ::	104	:: :: :: :: ::
5	:: :: :: :: ::	30	:: :: :: :: ::	55	:: :: :: :: ::	80	:: :: :: :: ::	105	:: :: :: :: ::
6	:: :: :: :: ::	31	:: :: :: :: ::	56	:: :: :: :: ::	81	:: :: :: :: ::	106	:: :: :: :: ::
7	:: :: :: :: ::	32	:: :: :: :: ::	57	:: :: :: :: ::	82	:: :: :: :: ::	107	:: :: :: :: ::
8	:: :: :: :: ::	33	:: :: :: :: ::	58	:: :: :: :: ::	83	:: :: :: :: ::	108	:: :: :: :: ::
9	:: :: :: :: ::	34	:: :: :: :: ::	59	:: :: :: :: ::	84	:: :: :: :: ::	109	:: :: :: :: ::
10	:: :: :: :: ::	35	:: :: :: :: ::	60	:: :: :: :: ::	85	:: :: :: :: ::	110	:: :: :: :: ::

Make only ONE mark for each answer.   Additional and stray marks may be
counted as mistakes.   In making corrections, erase errors COMPLETELY.

#	A B C D E	#	A B C D E	#	A B C D E	#	A B C D E	#	A B C D E
11	:: :: :: :: ::	36	:: :: :: :: ::	61	:: :: :: :: ::	86	:: :: :: :: ::	111	:: :: :: :: ::
12	:: :: :: :: ::	37	:: :: :: :: ::	62	:: :: :: :: ::	87	:: :: :: :: ::	112	:: :: :: :: ::
13	:: :: :: :: ::	38	:: :: :: :: ::	63	:: :: :: :: ::	88	:: :: :: :: ::	113	:: :: :: :: ::
14	:: :: :: :: ::	39	:: :: :: :: ::	64	:: :: :: :: ::	89	:: :: :: :: ::	114	:: :: :: :: ::
15	:: :: :: :: ::	40	:: :: :: :: ::	65	:: :: :: :: ::	90	:: :: :: :: ::	115	:: :: :: :: ::
16	:: :: :: :: ::	41	:: :: :: :: ::	66	:: :: :: :: ::	91	:: :: :: :: ::	116	:: :: :: :: ::
17	:: :: :: :: ::	42	:: :: :: :: ::	67	:: :: :: :: ::	92	:: :: :: :: ::	117	:: :: :: :: ::
18	:: :: :: :: ::	43	:: :: :: :: ::	68	:: :: :: :: ::	93	:: :: :: :: ::	118	:: :: :: :: ::
19	:: :: :: :: ::	44	:: :: :: :: ::	69	:: :: :: :: ::	94	:: :: :: :: ::	119	:: :: :: :: ::
20	:: :: :: :: ::	45	:: :: :: :: ::	70	:: :: :: :: ::	95	:: :: :: :: ::	120	:: :: :: :: ::
21	:: :: :: :: ::	46	:: :: :: :: ::	71	:: :: :: :: ::	96	:: :: :: :: ::	121	:: :: :: :: ::
22	:: :: :: :: ::	47	:: :: :: :: ::	72	:: :: :: :: ::	97	:: :: :: :: ::	122	:: :: :: :: ::
23	:: :: :: :: ::	48	:: :: :: :: ::	73	:: :: :: :: ::	98	:: :: :: :: ::	123	:: :: :: :: ::
24	:: :: :: :: ::	49	:: :: :: :: ::	74	:: :: :: :: ::	99	:: :: :: :: ::	124	:: :: :: :: ::
25	:: :: :: :: ::	50	:: :: :: :: ::	75	:: :: :: :: ::	100	:: :: :: :: ::	125	:: :: :: :: ::